ISSUES THAT CONCERN YOU

Sexual Harassment

*Arthur Gillard, **Book Editor***

GREENHAVEN PRESS
A part of Gale, Cengage Learning

GALE
CENGAGE Learning·

Detroit • New York • San Francisco • New Haven, Conn • Waterville, Maine • London

Elizabeth Des Chenes, *Director, Content Strategy*
Cynthia Sanner, *Publisher*
Douglas Dentino, *Manager, New Product*

Articles in Greenhaven Press anthologies are often edited for length to meet page requirements. In addition, original titles of these works are changed to clearly present the main thesis and to explicitly indicate the author's opinion. Every effort is made to ensure that Greenhaven Press accurately reflects the original intent of the authors. Every effort has been made to trace the owners of copyrighted material.

Cover image © Mohd Shahrizan Hussin/Shutterstock.com

LIBRARY OF CONGRESS CATALOGING-IN-PUBLICATION DATA
Sexual harassment / Arthur Gillard, book editor.
pages cm. -- (Issues that concern you)
Includes bibliographical references and index.
Audience: Age 14-18.
Audience: Grades 9-12.
ISBN 978-0-7377-6933-3 (hardcover)
1. Sexual harassment of women--United States--Juvenile literature. 2. Sexual harassment of men--United States--Juvenile literature. I. Gillard, Arthur.
HQ1237.5.U6S475 2014
305.3--dc23
2013042516

CONTENTS

Behaviors that today would be called sexual harassment have existed for a long time. But the term itself was not coined until 1975. It was used by a group of feminists working in the Human Relations Department at Cornell University who were helping a woman who had quit her job because she had been sexually harassed by her superior in one of Cornell's academic departments.

There are two basic categories of sexual harassment: (1) *quid pro quo* ("this for that"), in which someone is pressured to provide sexual favors in exchange for some benefit, such as a higher grade or a job promotion; and (2) *hostile environment*, in which unwelcome sexual comments or behaviors create an atmosphere that seriously interferes with someone's ability to do his or her job or schoolwork.

Advances in technology have lately altered the landscape of sexual harassment in a number of ways. New ways to interact—e-mail, chat, virtual worlds, texting, blogs, YouTube, etc.—while enriching people's lives in countless ways, have also provided new opportunities and "places" for sexual harassment. On the other hand, the fact that such interactions can easily be recorded has helped reveal the scope of the problem and has provided new possibilities for people who are targeted by sexual harassment to fight back. This increasingly includes the physical world as well because people use technology such as smartphones to record details of harassment incidents, which they can now publish on anti-sexual-harassment websites such as Hollaback! Or perhaps they use the Circle of 6 app for smartphones: Users of this award-winning app designate six friends who help each other in difficult situations, including sexual harassment or potentially violent confrontations. By pressing two buttons on their phones, users can send an alert to the six friends with automatic messages such as "Come and get me. I need help getting home safely" or "Call and pretend you need me. I need an interruption."

One area where these trends have converged is the online gaming community, which in 2012 experienced several prominent harassment cases that garnered enormous media attention. The cases highlighted the extent to which sexual harassment mars that community and creates a hostile environment for women. Although girls and women now make up nearly half of those who inhabit online gaming's virtual world, that world has traditionally been considered a predominantly male domain, with games and marketing designed to appeal to young males—for example, by using hypersexualized images of women in many games and advertisements. As in many other historical cases of women entering traditionally male domains, such as the business world, women seeking to participate in the gaming community have often initially been greeted by sexual harassment and hostility.

The website NKA: Not in the Kitchen Anymore, created by Jenny Haniver, features many audio clips illustrating the sexual harassment she experiences daily as a woman playing online games featuring real-time player interaction. Comments directed at her by male players range from gendered insults to sexual come-ons, insults, and threats of rape. Another website, Fat, Ugly or Slutty, takes a humorous approach to the problem, posting screenshots of text messages sent to female gamers, along with mocking commentary by the website's editors. The posts are divided into self-explanatory categories such as "Lewd Proposals," "Slutty," "X-Rated," and "Death Threats." (The name "Fat, Ugly, or Slutty" derives from three common labels applied to women who play video games.) According to pop culture critic and game designer Anita Sarkeesian, the underlying motivation of such attacks is "maintaining and reinforcing and normalizing a culture of sexism where men who harass are supported by their peers and rewarded for their sexist attitudes and behaviors, and where women are silenced, marginalized and excluded from full participation. A boy's club means no girls allowed. And how do they keep women and girls out? Just like this: by creating an environment that is too toxic and hostile to endure."[1]

Sarkeesian has herself been the target of online sexual harassment. But when she launched a Kickstarter fund-raising campaign

New ways to interact—e-mail, chat, virtual worlds, texting, blogs, YouTube, etc.—in addition to enriching people's lives have also provided new opportunities for sexual harassment.

to raise money for a series of videos examining sexist stereotypes and negative portrayals of women in video games, she was unprepared for the level of sexual harassment and gender-based attacks directed at her by a vocal minority of angry men who saw her as a threat to "their" gaming culture. Some of the many instances of online harassment she experienced include her Wikipedia page being defaced with sexist and racist slurs and pornographic imagery; rape threats; cartoons posted online and sent to her e-mail that depict her being raped by video game characters; and misogynist attacks in comments to her YouTube videos (two of the milder examples being "tits or gtfo" [get the f- -k out] and "Back to the kitchen, c- -t"). One enraged gamer even designed an interactive video game called "Beat Up Anita Sarkeesian" that used a photoshopped image of her being progressively battered and bloodied as the player clicked on her face. Far from silencing her, the attacks resulted in supporters pledging far more money for her project than she was originally asking for, greatly expanding the project's scope (see www.feministfrequency.com/tag/tropes -vs-women-in-video-games/ for more details).

Games, and the way people play them, reflect the values and realities of the culture at large (albeit in exaggerated, dreamlike form), which is what makes Sarkeesian's pop culture critiques of sexist and misogynist themes in video games so interesting. Another provocative project is the game "Hey Baby" by Suyin Looui. Designed in part as a satire of popular first-person shooter games, "Hey Baby" allows the player to experience being a woman walking city streets populated by men who accost her with various forms of harassment, ranging from seemingly innocuous greetings to lewd comments and rape threats. The player can respond either by saying, "Thanks, have a great day" or by blasting the harasser with a machine gun. Looui was inspired to create the game in response to street harassment she has experienced. She wanted to create a satirical game that humorously exaggerated revenge fantasies women have in response to sexual harassment. Although many commentators decried the violence in the game, Looui was surprised to find many men supporting it: "I've had really amaz-ing emails and blog posts from male players who have shared it with their friends because they thought it was important,"[2] she notes. *New York Times* game reviewer Seth Schiesel found himself initially disturbed by the antimale violence in "Hey Baby," but as he continued to play he felt an increasing appreciation for what many women experience as they go about their lives. He also discovered that nothing he did would ever stop the harassment. "I found myself throwing up my hands and thinking, 'Well what am I supposed to do?' Which is, of course, what countless women think every day."[3]

The viewpoints in this anthology offer a variety of perspectives on sexual harassment. In addition, the volume contains several appendixes that help the reader understand and explore the topic further, including a thorough bibliography and a list of organizations to contact for more information. The appendix titled "What You Should Know About Sexual Harassment" offers facts about the subject that can be used in debates and essays. The appendix "What You Should Do About Sexual Harassment" offers advice for young people who are concerned with doing something about sexual harassment. With all these features, *Issues That Concern You: Sexual Harassment* provides an excellent resource for everyone interested in this timely topic.

Notes

1. Anita Sarkeesian, "TEDxWomen Talk About Online Harassment & Cyber Mobs," Feminist Frequency, December 5, 2012. www.feministfrequency.com/2012/12/tedxwomen-talk-on-sexist-harassment-cyber-mobs.
2. Games for Change, "Interview with 'Hey Baby' Creator Suyin Looui," February 16, 2011. www.gamesforchange.org/2011/02/interview-with-hey-baby-creator-suyin-looui.
3. Seth Schiesel, "A Woman with the Firepower to Silence Those Street Wolves," *New York Times*, June 7, 2010. www.nytimes.com/2010/06/08/arts/television/08baby.html?_r=0.

ONE

An Overview of Sexual Harassment

Megan Maguire

Megan Maguire has a master's degree in educational psychology from Rutgers, the State University of New Jersey. In the following viewpoint Maguire discusses the problem of sexual harassment in schools that occurs between school staff and students or between students. Although more attention is paid to teacher-on-student harassment, the author contends, studies have found that harassment between students is more common. According to Maguire, sexual harassment can be any unwanted sexual behavior, whether verbal (e.g., comments, jokes), nonverbal (e.g., displaying pornography), or physical (e.g., touching, pulling at clothes, rape). The Civil Rights Act of 1964 prohibits sexual harassment in the workplace; in 1972 it was extended to protect students. The author notes that sexual harassment can have significantly adverse effects, including depression, self-doubt, and declines in academic performance. Schools have a responsibility to protect students, but this can be challenging because sexual harassment often goes unreported or even unrecognized, the author claims.

Megan Maguire, "Sexual Harassment," as in *Encyclopedia of Cross-Cultural School Psychology*, ed. Caroline S. Clauss-Ehlers, 2010, pp. 884–887, with kind permission from Springer Science+Business MEdia B.V.

Sexual harassment is an issue that plagues the schools of our nation. Sexual harassment occurs in our school systems between school personnel (i.e., teachers and administrators) and students as well as between students. Previously, sexual harassment between teachers and students has received the most attention. However, much attention has recently been given to student-to-student sexual harassment. Recent studies show that sexual harassment occurs much more often between students than it does with the teacher as the aggressor. In a representative study of the U.S., 87% of female students and 71% of male students reported being the victim of sexual harassment at the hands of other students. Another study revealed that 80% of adolescent students report that they have been the victim of sexual harassment by their peers. This is in contrast to the 20% of female students and 8% of male students who report sexual harassment at the hands of their teachers. The aggressors of sexual harassment, whether it is student-on-student or teacher-on-student, are typically male. In fact, studies have shown that the perpetrators tend to be males regardless of the sex of the victim.

Sexual Harassment Defined

There is a very large spectrum of what is considered to be sexual harassment. Sexual harassment is considered to be any form of unwelcome behavior of a sexual nature. Forms of sexual harassment fall into three categories. These categories: physical, verbal, and nonverbal. Physical sexual harassment is typically perceived to be the most severe form of harassment. Physical sexual harassment is any form of unwanted physical contact. This includes unwanted touching, unwelcome sexual advances, pulling at clothing, sexual assault, or even rape. Verbal sexual assault includes requests for sexual favors, comments about body parts, sexual jokes or invitations, and any other inappropriate comments of a sexual nature. Nonverbal sexual harassment includes showing pornographic materials or cornering an individual in a sexually threatening manner.

Verbal harassment is the type of sexual harassment that occurs between students most frequently. School personnel, on the other hand, seem to commit nonverbal and physical sexual harassment most frequently. Sexual harassment also differs by the gender of the victim. Female students tend to report being the victim of nonverbal and physical harassment more than male students. Male students report more verbal harassment than do female students.

Legal Issues

Students are protected from sexual harassment under the Civil Rights Act of 1964. This act was initially put into legislation to protect victims of sexual harassment in the workplace. In 1972 the act was amended to extend its protection to those in an educational program. The U.S. Department of Education's Office of Civil Rights offered a new definition of sexual harassment in 1997. According to Title IX (Education Amendments act of 1972) sexual harassment is defined as behavior that is sufficiently severe, persistent, or pervasive so that it adversely affects a student's education or creates a hostile or abusive educational environment and the conduct must be sexual in nature.

This law also states that schools will be held responsible in the situation that sexual harassment is knowingly occurring between students, yet the school does not act to protect students. A school can be sued for its failure to protect students from teacher-on-student, as well as student-on-student sexual harassment. Schools are required to award monetary compensation to the victims of sexual harassment. One such example is the 1992 case of *Franklin v. Gwinnett County Public Schools*. Here the U.S. Supreme Court ruled that a school district would pay monetary damages to a student who was sexually harassed by her teacher. In the 1999 case of *Davis v. Monroe County Board of Education*, the U.S. Supreme Court ruled in favor of the plaintiff. The board of education was required to pay damages to the victim of student-on-student sexual harassment. In the *Davis* case, school officials were aware of the harassment but failed to act upon the reported events. Under

Title IX, it is the responsibility of a school district to develop and implement a policy against sexual harassment. These policies should outline the grievance procedures to be followed when instances of sexual harassment occur.

Effect on Students

Sexual harassment creates a very hostile environment where academic and personal development is severely hindered. Victims of sexual harassment may display symptoms of depression, engage in self blame, experience helplessness, self-doubt, and avoid school.

Sexual harassment elicits a wide variety of emotional responses from the victim. A common response is fear. The Hostile Hallways study was commissioned by the American Association of

Sexual harassment is an issue in US schools, occurring between school personnel and students as well as between students themselves.

University Women and looked at the effect of the school climate on female students. According to the Hostile Hallways study, a third of students fear being sexually harassed in school. Fear also prevents students from reporting sexual harassment. Sexual harassment also affects the student's sense of identity. Seventeen percent of students in the Hostile Hallways study reported a feeling of identity confusion following their harassment.

Victims of sexual harassment often experience a decline in academic performance. The Hostile Hallways study found that victims of sexual harassment do not want to attend school as a result of the harassment. Victims are also likely to avoid participating in classroom activities to discourage further attention from the harasser. All of this contributes to the academic decline following the experience of being sexually harassed.

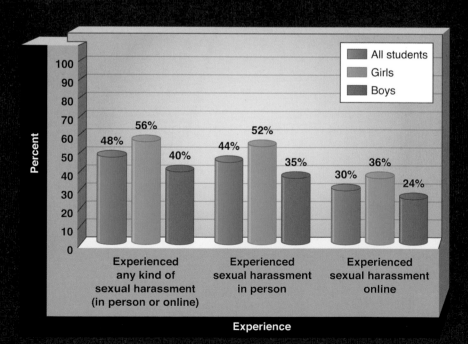

Students Who Experienced Sexual Harassment During the 2010–2011 School Year, by Gender

Legend:
- All students
- Girls
- Boys

Experienced any kind of sexual harassment (in person or online): 48%, 56%, 40%

Experienced sexual harassment in person: 44%, 52%, 35%

Experienced sexual harassment online: 30%, 36%, 24%

y-axis: Percent (0 to 100)
x-axis: Experience

Taken from: Catherine Hill and Holly Kearl. *Crossing the Line: Sexual Harassment at School*, AAUW, November 2011. www.aauw.org/research/crossing-the-line/.

While both male and female students are negatively affected by harassment, it appears that male and female students react differently to it. Girls tend to report feeling more fear as a result of the harassment in comparison to their male counterparts. Female students also report more feelings of embarrassment, self-consciousness, and lack of confidence more so than their male counterparts.

Difficulties of Attacking Sexual Harassment

Sexual harassment is a difficult issue to attack in that it is very seldom reported. Students are very reluctant to report instances of unwelcome sexual attention. One study found that only 56% of students that experience sexual harassment share their experiences with another person. In the Hostile Hallways study less than 10% of victimized students reported the harassment to an adult within the school. Less than a quarter of the victimized students reported the harassment to their families. Victims are more likely to report the harassment to a friend. Additionally 63% of the students in the Hostile Hallways study reported their harassment to a friend. This study also found that 23% of students did not report their harassment to anyone.

Another difficulty that has been encountered in attempts to address sexual harassment is the ambiguity of student-on-student sexual harassment. Harassment perpetrated by a teacher toward a student is more easily identified as the different power status is easily visible. Teacher-on-student sexual harassment is more likely to be reported than peer sexual harassment. However, as there is no power difference between students it is difficult to deem what behavior is to be considered sexual harassment and what behavior is "normal" for adolescents. Physically intrusive behavior is more often identified as sexual harassment than is nonphysically intrusive behavior. Students are more likely to perceive inappropriate touching as sexual harassment than they would jokes of a sexual nature.

What Schools Can Do

It is the responsibility of the school district and the professionals within the school to protect students from sexual harassment.

This responsibility extends beyond uncovering and reporting occurrences of harassment. Schools must provide a nonhostile environment for students. Teachers and other professionals must be educated about detecting and handling sexual harassment. On a curriculum level, schools must develop a nonsexist environment. This means that only nonsexist teaching methods will be employed.

Schools must also prepare and educate students about what should be done in the case that they are a victim. Many students are not fully aware of behaviors that constitute sexual harassment. Students need guidance in determining which behaviors are mere flirting and what behavior is harassing. Another area in which student education can help deter harassment is empowerment. Students with a heightened sense of empowerment are less likely to tolerate harassment and more likely to report. Teachers, counselors, and principles must make students aware that harassment will not be tolerated and that they will be protected. Students should be aware of the resources that are available if they are the victims of sexual harassment.

Lastly schools must create an effective antiharassment policy in which student reports are responded to effectively. Students, teachers, parents, and administrators must all be familiar with this policy. This policy should address the issue of confidentiality. Many students fear the repercussions of reporting harassment. Students must be ensured that their reports will be kept as confidential as possible, that they do not need to face the accused harasser, and that the victim will always be protected. This policy should also make clear the consequences of sexual harassment to the individual doing the harassment.

TWO

Why Men Can't— and Shouldn't—Stop Staring at Women

Ian Brown

> Ian Brown is a feature writer for the Toronto newspaper the *Globe and Mail*, and editor of *What I Meant to Say: The Private Lives of Men*. In the following viewpoint Brown argues that men staring at women in the street is a completely natural and unavoidable behavior. He shares his own experience of the "male gaze" and discusses the phenomenon with various other men and women. The people he quotes generally see nothing wrong with simply looking at women in the street, although some distinctions are made between *looking* and *leering* (with the latter considered unacceptable), and one woman notes that while she does not object to men merely looking at women in the street, sexual comments from men are offensive to her.

Before we discuss why it is men can't and shouldn't stop looking at women in the street, I'd like to explain about the girl in the miniskirt on the bicycle.

It was the first of the warm spring days that inflated Toronto this week. I was on my way to work on my bicycle. Two blocks from my house, I turned right and found myself 10 feet behind a young woman.

I use the word "behind" hesitantly.

She might have been 20. I am 58. She had long blond hair, and was wearing a short putty-coloured jacket, nude hose—I didn't think anyone wore nude hose any more—and a white miniskirt, trim but straining, tucked primly beneath her.

My first sight of her felt like a light blow to the chest. Her body held my interest, but so did her decision to wear a miniskirt on a bike, along with her youth, her loveliness, even the fleetingness of the six blocks I kept her company—she turned right, and she was gone. We owed each other nothing.

The inevitable backwash of guilt arrived, as all men know it does. I have a daughter her age. I am married but spent several minutes gazing at a pretty girl's backside. I could hear the charges: objectifier, perv, pig, *man*.

But it was such a beautiful day. And so I decided to spend the rest of it cruising the city, investigating the famous male gaze, to find out just how ashamed we lads ought to feel. These days, with women charging so fast past us, we're happy to feel anything.

Details that catch my attention: lively calves, French blue puff skirts with white polka dots, red shoes, dark skin, olive skin, pale skin, lips (various shapes), curly hair (to my surprise). A pretty girl with too much bottom squeezed into her yoga pants—and, mysteriously, twice as sexy for the effort. A slim blond in enormous sunglasses carrying a banana peel as if it were a memo. An expensively dressed and tanned woman climbs out of a taxi, so vivacious I panic and can't look at her. Slim girls, curvy girls; signs of health, hints of quiet style. Coloured headbands. A rollerblader in white short shorts does nothing for me: Her look is the sexual equivalent of shopping at Wal-Mart.

But each woman makes you think, parse her appeal. The busty brunette in her 20s is wearing a rich emerald-green ruffled blouse, but it's sleeveless and obviously not warm enough to wear outside. Is she a bad planner? Would she be a sloppy mate?

I ask a woman sitting in an outdoor cafe if she minds being looked at by men. Her name is Ali—a 26-year-old student with an Italian boyfriend who looks at everyone. That used to bother her but doesn't any more. "Just looking, I don't think it's offensive. But I think it's offensive if there's comments."

Every woman I speak to says the same thing, without exception. So why does girl-watching have such a terrible reputation? Maybe because it's an act of rebellion.

X meets me for lunch at Ki, a downtown sushi restaurant frequented by brokers and lawyers. A big-time lawyer married to the same woman for three decades, he's father to three children—the opposite of a player. But he, too, spends hours gazing at women. He claims he spots at least two stunners a day. We've been discussing the girl on the bicycle.

"I don't get this complaint that you can't look at an attractive woman who's the same age as your 20-year-old daughter," X says.

I'm having a hard time concentrating: Ki's waitresses are brain-stopping. Cleavage seems to be the *prix fixe*. One of them catches me looking at her, and then catches me looking sheepishly away, my store of hope fading the way a car battery dies. But a little bit of shame is good: you can't take your gandering for granted.

"It's because you could be her father," I finally manage to say.

"Yeah," X replies. "But you're not."

He pauses. "I read that 26 is the peak of a woman's sexual attractiveness. I've got a daughter who's 26—so I can't find someone that age attractive? That strikes me as a creepy argument. Women might not credit that a man can look at someone of that age without lust, but as the father of someone that age, I can."

X believes men look at attractive women because attractiveness means the women are healthy, an evolutionary advantage.

"That's still seems unfair to the less attractive," I point out.

"And it bites women a lot harder than it bites men. I'm conscious of it being unfair. But there's nothing I can do about it."

"We could stop looking."

"Would that help anything?"

"That's not an answer. Could you stop looking?"

"You'd have to pretty much turn out the lights."

The trick is to look and keep what you see to yourself.

There are people sunning themselves all over downtown Toronto, glades of flesh and sunglasses. Ninety per cent of them are women. It's not as if they're hiding.

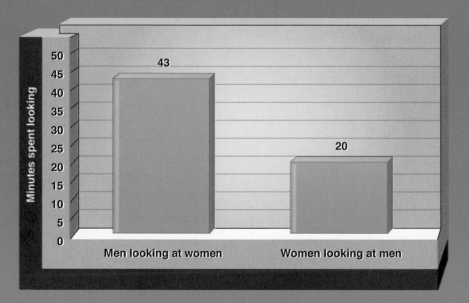

Amount of Time Men and Women Spend Staring at Each Other per Day

According to a poll of three thousand people conducted by Kodak Lens Vision Centres in the United Kingdom, men (on average) spend twice as much time per day admiring the physical attractiveness of women as women spend admiring men.

Taken from: "Men Spend a Year Staring at Women." *Telegraph* (UK), August 4, 2009. www.telegraph.co.uk/news/newstopics/howaboutthat/5970007/Men–spend–a–year–staring–at–women.html.

On the co-ed-strewn quad of Victoria College at the University of Toronto, I run into K, a businesswoman I know. She's here studying for a night course. She just turned 50, and is still attractive. But she admits looks from men are rarer. "Leering hasn't happened in years," she adds wistfully. Visiting Italy 20 years ago with friends, "we were furious that the Italian men pinched your bum. When we went back, in our early 40s, we were furious that no one was pinching our bums." This makes me as sad as it seems to make her.

She points out there is a difference between a look and a leer and disagrees with X's rule that eye contact with a passing woman can last no more than one second.

"Well, I'd say two or three seconds. A lingering look, especially if it's from an Adonis—that's, *oooh*. And you never see them again. A passing encounter. Or a bus encounter, glances and sidelong looks until one of you gets off the bus? That's the best."

The first time she stepped out of the library this morning into the quad of semi-clad women, "I thought to myself, oh my god, do you remember what it was like to be able to expose your legs? It wasn't even sexual. But it was liberating."

This is another thing that made the girl on the bike so appealing: she was free. It would be nice if we all were. Y, a 35-year-old married friend who still flicks his gaze at passing women the way other people flip channels, blames our national earnestness. "The problem for us as men is that we're in the wrong culture, and we're men at the wrong time. We're not a culture that empowers men with casual sensuality."

He holds up his BlackBerry. "I don't see what's wrong with it. In a world where, thanks to this thing, I am only two clicks away from double penetration and other forms of pornographic nastiness, the act of merely looking at a girl who is naturally pretty—I mean, we should celebrate that."

It's nearly dinnertime when I make my last stop at L'Espresso, an Italian café near my house. Even here, on a quiet patio at the end of the day, I can see five women I want to look at. It's almost, but not quite, exhausting.

Then I notice W and Z at the patio's corner table—the best view in the place. Both men are in their early 60s, both married. They're surprisingly keen to discuss the male gaze.

"Yes, I look at girls still, incessantly and unavoidably," says W, the taller of the two. He still has a full mane of tossed-back hair. "And it's one of my greatest pleasures in life."

"I concur," Z says. Z is shorter, less ephemeral. "But I look and gaze at all women in the street, whether they're beauties or not. They're all interesting. And different men gaze at different women."

"And what goes through your mind when you look at them?" I ask. "Do you think, would I sleep with her, and what does that say about me?"

"Yes, there is a question," Z says, "but for me the question as I look at them is a little more modest: Would *they* sleep with *me?*"

"Beautiful women are like flowers," W interjects. "They turn to the sun. But if they don't receive a certain amount of attention, they wither." The simile has an 18th-century feel, like the conversation: It's about manners, after all, which are always most complicated in times of equality.

"I concur again," Z says. "The most attractive women expect an attentive gaze that doesn't imply anything other than someone saying, 'You're attractive enough to gaze at.' And the most rewarding thing is if that gaze is returned."

"What does a returned glance imply?" I ask.

"It implies, as they say in the New York State lottery: You never know."

The author argues that men staring at women in the street is a completely natural and unavoidable behavior.

I'm about to leave when Z tosses me a last thought. "Some women assume the male gaze is sinful and hurtful and evil, that men can never look at women in a different way. But that's not what the gaze is about. Because a sophisticated man would not hesitate to gaze, and then he might be filled with regret and loss, and therefore gain self-knowledge."

Longing makes us sad, but at least it proves we're still alive. Which is why men like spring so much, for the short time it lasts.

THREE

Sexual Harassment Is About Power, Not Desire

Eric Anthony Grollman

Eric Anthony Grollman is a doctoral candidate in sociology at Indiana University. His research interests include sexuality and issues of race, gender, and class. In the following viewpoint Grollman argues that sexual harassment is a sexualized expression of power over an oppressed group. He gives examples such as heterosexual men harassing other men, and gay men sexually harassing women, that raise questions about whether the underlying motivation behind such behaviors is really sexual desire, as is commonly assumed. According to the author, although sexual harassment is *often* motivated by men expressing power over women, it also occurs in cases of racism, homophobia, and other forms of discrimination. Because of the limitations of how people view sexual harassment, such cases often go unrecognized and unpunished. Grollman suggests that the definition of sexual harassment needs to be broadened so that all sexualized expressions of oppressive power will be dealt with appropriately.

Eric Anthony Grollman, "What Is Sexual Harassment? A Different Perspective," *Kinsey Confidential*, October 15, 2012. http://kinseyconfidential.org. Copyright © 2012 by The Kinsey Institute. All rights reserved. Reproduced by permission.

Think about this story for a moment:

In November [2009], . . . the Cheesecake Factory restaurant chain agreed to pay $345,000 to six male employees who claimed they were repeatedly sexually assaulted by a group of male kitchen staffers at a Phoenix-area restaurant.

Okay, now let me share another story with you:

. . . but one thing I noticed about him was that he feels up every woman he meets.

The first story came from an MSNBC article about the rising number of men filing formal claims of sexual harassment in the workplace. The second story is a critique of a character on "The Real Housewives of Atlanta." Who is a gay man: can gay men sexually harass straight women? I bet that there is a good chance that after reading the first story, you thought to yourself, "oh, the male perpetrators must be gay!" And, after reading the second, you might have caught yourself questioning how a gay man could sexually harass a woman—why would he want to?

The point of this exercise is to highlight that many of us assume, even subconsciously, that sexual harassment entails some unwanted and harassing behaviors motivated by *sexual desire*. So, some might find it confusing that a heterosexual person would harass someone of their same gender, or that a gay man might harass a woman. But, what underlies sexual harassment is an expression of power—not desire.

Sexual Harassment as a Gendered Expression of Power

Beginning with the US Civil Rights Act of 1964, the dominant, legal definition of sexual harassment that has evolved over time is one of harassing behaviors or differential treatment that are sexual in nature. This includes unwanted sexual advances, requests for sexual favors, and creating a hostile environment. While it is

Sexual harassment includes unwanted sexual advances, requests for sexual favors, and creating a hostile environment.

understood that men can also be the victims of sexual harassment, men as harassers and women as targets of harassment is central to our common understanding of sexual harassment. In fact, sexual harassment is commonly defined as a form of gender-based discrimination (against women).

There is a great deal of work, particularly in the social sciences, women and gender studies, and sexuality studies that demonstrates that sexual harassment is an expression of power, especially along the lines of gender. For example, three sociologists recently published a study in which they found that women who hold supervisor-level positions are more likely than women who do not to experience sexual harassment. These experiences for women supervisors largely serve to put them "in their place," signaling that they are unwelcome in a position of power *as women*. Unfortunately, factors beyond interactions among individuals appear to place women at greater risk for harassment working in male-dominated fields, and being physically and socially isolated from other women.

Sexual Harassment Is Not (Only) About Gender

Indeed, women are not alone in being targets of sexual harassment. Though less common, some men are victims of these experiences, as well. In another sociological study on sexual harassment, a number of men reported experiencing sexually harassing behaviors: however, men are much more apprehensive to define these experiences as sexual harassment, probably because the common understanding limits these experiences to women. This study also pointed out two interesting dynamics: adolescent males and men who are financially vulnerable (i.e., feel they do not have control over their financial situation) are more frequently targets of sexual harassment.

Indeed, sexual harassment is not merely a gendered phenomenon. For example, there has been a great deal of attention in research to racial differences in women's experiences of sexual harassment. This work has explored whether women of color are more often targeted than white women, [whether] there are racial differences in defining one's experiences as harassment, and whether women of color *experience* sexual harassment differently than white women. Some Black feminist scholars like Patricia Hill Collins and Angela Y. Davis have noted that sexual harassment and other forms of sexual violence are manifestations of sexism, *as well as* racism and classism [discrimination based on social status].

But, I wish to push this perspective one step further—sexual harassment is the sexual-based expression of any system of oppression, be it sexism, racism, homophobia or heterosexism, transphobia [fear of transgendered people], classism, ableism [discrimination against disabled people], ageism, fatphobia, or xenophobia [fear of foreigners]. A few examples come to mind:

- A white heterosexual man jokes with his Black heterosexual male coworker that he must have a large penis (because he's Black).
- A heterosexual woman doctor asks a lesbian patient about the particular sexual activities in which she engages with her female sexual partners to make sense of why the patient does not regularly use (male) condoms or other forms of birth control.
- A girl from a working-class background is teased frequently by boys at her school that she provides oral sex in the school bathroom to make money. . . .

A Different Perspective

So, two related points come from this perspective on sexual harassment. Sexual harassment is not limited to the unwanted and harassing behaviors that are sexual in nature by (heterosexual) men targeted toward (heterosexual) [women]. To focus just on gender and, specifically on men as harassers and women as victims, forces us to overlook the other various ways in which sexual harassment occurs. As a consequence, many people whose experiences fall outside of this traditional view may fail to define their experiences as sexual harassment, leading them to forgo seeking legal recourse or protection, or any actions to end the harassment in general.

The other related point is that this male-harasser-female-victim perspective is somewhat heterosexist; that is, it presumes that all parties involved are heterosexual. By extension, this means that heterosexual desire must be present—one that entails a sexually aggressive heterosexual man and a sexually-disinterested heterosexual woman. I must state this clearly, here: *sexual harassment is not an expression of desire*. As such, one individual may repeatedly sexually harass another individual whom they do not find sexually desirable. In the case of sexual harassment between men, for example, it is probably the case that heterosexual men sexually harass gay men much more frequently than the reverse.)

Percentage of College Students Who Have Been Sexually Harassed, by Sexual Identity

LGBT (lesbian, gay, bisexual, and transgender) college students are significantly more likely to experience sexual harassment than their heterosexual peers, according to a study done in 2005 by the American Association of University Women (AAUW).

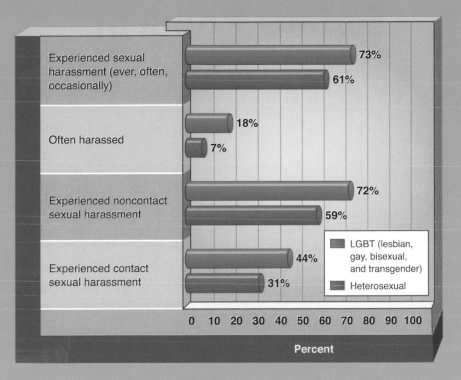

Taken from: C. Hill and E. Silva. *Drawing the Line: Sexual Harassment on Campus*, AAUW Educational Foundation, 2005. www.aauw.org/resource/drawing–the–line–sexual–harassment–on–campus/.

Now that US laws have shifted to reflect the reality that some men are survivors of sexual violence, it may be time to broaden how we define sexual harassment. Indeed, we are beginning to acknowledge that men, too, are targets of sexual harassment. But, it may be necessary that we recognize that sexual harassment may be an expression of racism, heterosexism, sexism, transphobia, classism, or any other form of oppression—as well as the intersections among them.

FOUR

Sexual Harassment in School Is a Serious Problem

Elizabeth J. Meyer

Elizabeth J. Meyer is the author of *Gender, Bullying, and Harassment: Strategies to End Sexism and Homophobia in Schools*. In the following viewpoint Meyer argues that schools have a high rate of sexual harassment, with harmful effects on those who experience it. She discusses a case where a student named Phoebe Prince experienced repeated sexual harassment, culminating in her suicide. Prince's school was taking steps to deal with bullying but had not addressed the problem of sexual harassment, which reflects a common pattern, according to the author. Meyer asserts that young women face an impossible dilemma in being pressured to be both sexually appealing to boys *and* not considered a "slut" by other girls. She suggests that girls need to take control of their own sexuality, including the right to choose not to have sex, and that teachers and school administrators need to deal more actively with sexual harassment.

I must confess that I am a true "Gleek" [fan of the TV show *Glee*]! I particularly loved this week's [in April 2010] Madonna-themed episode. Not only did it have fantastic music and dancing, it took on the very important topic of empowering young women and educating young men to be more sensitive and respectful of their female peers. It all started when Mr. Schuester overheard his student, Rachel, asking her peers for advice on how to handle pressure from guys for sex. Finding the perfect balance between the Madonna/whore [in this instance "Madonna" refers to the image of the Virgin Mary] extremes is an impossible act for most women to navigate, let alone teenagers who are subject to peer pressure and lack important access to unbiased resources and accurate information about sexuality. This desire to be sexually appealing to one's male peers but not seen as a slut by one's female peers was also at play in the last few months of Phoebe Prince's life in South Hadley, Massachusetts.

Sexual Pressure and Sexual Empowerment

In this week's episode of *Glee*, Mr. Schuester assigns his students to find Madonna songs in the hopes of empowering his female students with her message of strength and independence.

Lawyers for three teenagers accused of bullying Phoebe Prince appear in court on April 16, 2010. Prince endured months of harassment from the students before committing suicide.

Although I loved the show, using Madonna to empower young women is somewhat problematic since so much of her commercial success and cultural impact was directly tied to her overtly sexual costumes, dancing, and lyrics. This may send the message to young women that sexual equality can be obtained, but only if you "own" your sexuality by being the initiator rather than the receiver or rejector of sexual contact. This played out in 3 different vignettes of female characters inviting a male object of desire to have sex (all while singing "Like a Virgin," of course). Fortunately, this sequence ended with two characters opting out—which allowed another narrative to emerge: you can own your body and be empowered by deciding when you are ready and by not giving in to others' expectations of when you 'should' have sex, not just by initiating sex.

How does this relate to Phoebe Prince? Most of the headlines that have been written about her tragic death [in 2010] have linked her suicide to the "bullying" she experienced over several months at her new high school. . . . Although she was definitely bullied by being exposed repeatedly and over time to negative actions that were intended to hurt the target . . . , most of the "negative actions" that were directed at her were sexual in nature. She was repeatedly called, "Irish slut" and "ho." The origins of these insults were linked to her brief sexual relationships with two older guys and the jealousy that followed from the girls these boys had [had] previous relationships with. Although many are horrified with the lack of action taken by the school to stop this behaviour and protect Phoebe, it is sadly consistent with the current research on sexual harassment in schools.

Sexual Harassment Is More Harmful than Bullying Is

Over the past 15 years several studies have documented the prevalence and public nature of sexual harassment in schools. . . . In [researcher G.] Timmerman's (2003) study she found that sexual harassment happened so regularly (both student-student and teacher-student) that the only explanation for this was that the

Student Suggestions for Reducing Sexual Harassment at School, by Gender

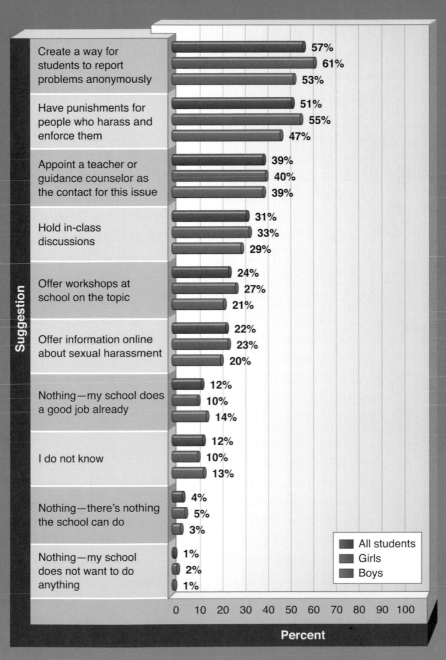

Suggestion

| Create a way for students to report problems anonymously | 57% / 61% / 53% |

- Create a way for students to report problems anonymously: 57%, 61%, 53%
- Have punishments for people who harass and enforce them: 51%, 55%, 47%
- Appoint a teacher or guidance counselor as the contact for this issue: 39%, 40%, 39%
- Hold in-class discussions: 31%, 33%, 29%
- Offer workshops at school on the topic: 24%, 27%, 21%
- Offer information online about sexual harassment: 22%, 23%, 20%
- Nothing—my school does a good job already: 12%, 10%, 14%
- I do not know: 12%, 10%, 13%
- Nothing—there's nothing the school can do: 4%, 5%, 3%
- Nothing—my school does not want to do anything: 1%, 2%, 1%

0 10 20 30 40 50 60 70 80 90 100

Percent

Legend: All students / Girls / Boys

Taken from: Catherine Hill and Holly Kearl. *Crossing the Line: Sexual Harassment at School.* AAUW, November 2012. www.aauw.org/research/crossing–the–line/.

culture of the school accepts this behaviour as normal. In [J.E.] Gruber & [S.] Fineran's (2008) study that compared bullying and sexual harassment, they found that although bullying was more pervasive, sexual harassment had more severe impacts on the self-esteem, mental & physical health of targeted students, and that girls and GLBT [gay, lesbian, bisexual, and transgender] students were more often targeted. In my own research . . . I reported that teachers hesitated to intervene in cases of sexual and homophobic harassment because they lacked clear leadership from their administration on these issues and were afraid of professional and parental backlash for taking on such 'controversial' topics.

Sadly, the teachers and administrators at South Hadley were doing what most professional educators do: they were talking about bullying, but completely ignoring sexual harassment. They had already had Barbara Coloroso (author of *The Bully, the Bullied, and the Bystander*) in to address their school and were starting an anti-bullying task force. These actions will work to reduce certain kinds of bullying, but unless sexual harassment and homophobia are explicitly named and talked about, students like Phoebe will continue to suffer in silence and the culture of the school (which is created by students, teachers, and the community within which it is situated) will continue to teach girls to live in the impossible patriarchal sexist roles of either Madonna or whore and teach boys to be sexist macho womanizers.

This is why I love *Glee*. This show paints a portrait of the social hierarchies in high school and the ways different teachers either reinforce (Sue Sylvester) or try to work against them (Will Schuester). Near the end of this episode, Mr. Schuester had his male students sing "What it feels like for a girl." These lyrics helped a few of the guys reflect on how they had been treating their female peers and led to some improvements in their relationships. Let's hope there are a few more Mr. Schuesters out there sharing these important lessons about gender equality and respect with their students so we don't have many more stories that end like Phoebe Prince's did.

FIVE

PC Police Target Middle and High School Students

Paul Gottfried

Paul Gottfried is a former professor of humanities at Elizabethtown College, in Pennsylvania, and author of nine books, including *Multiculturalism and the Politics of Guilt* and *Conservatism in America: Making Sense of the American Right*. In the following viewpoint Gottfried argues that efforts to solve the problem of sexual harassment in schools constitute excessive interference by the government in people's lives. Although he believes that students should be punished by teachers for making hurtful remarks, he says that using legal and governmental mechanisms to rigidly enforce rules creates more harm than it is intended to prevent. For example, Gottfried claims that it is far too easy under the current system for a woman offended by a look or comment to sue, causing great damage with little risk to herself—i.e., she could make a lot of money if she wins the lawsuit, but would face no serious consequences if she loses, whereas the accused would suffer permanent harm no matter what the outcome.

The PC police are at it again. According to a sympathetic Associated Press report on November 7 and a survey conducted by the American Association of University Women, "sexual harassment is pervasive in grades 7–12." Such improprieties are taking place "in person or electronically via texting, email and social media," and those issuing and summarizing the report think that the offenses are serious enough to require political action. Harassment, by the way, includes "having someone make unwelcome sexual comments" and "the taunting of youth perceived to be gay or lesbian." A spokeswoman from the National Women's Law Center explains that the "ultimate goal" in the crusade against harassing speech "should be to deter hurtful student interactions however they are defined."

The last phrase may be basic for understanding the report. The groups that prepared it favor using state power to monitor speech in both public and private educational facilities. Students and teachers are to be apprised of the government's sexual harassment policy and the young should "be educated about what their rights are under Title IX (banning any form of gender discrimination), with special attention paid to encouraging girls to respond assertively to harassment because they are targeted more often than boys." Moreover, an official for the National Association of Secondary School Principals indicates that bigotry has become dangerously hidden in recent years. Instead of "overt attempts" to make sexual advances, we now have "more use of sexual remarks to degrade or insult someone."

There is nothing novel about these concerns. We have been living for decades with expanding government surveillance over our minds and emotions, a development that I describe in my books as "the triumph of the therapeutic state." Sadly the outcry against this tyranny has been so underwhelming that I expect it to go on and on into the distant future. Universities and corporations are already being forced to monitor selectively insensitive speech (such as straights insulting gays but not the reverse), and about twenty years ago I began to notice that men hanging out in gyms were looking over their shoulders lest they be overheard engaging in "hurtful interactions." Should we therefore expect any limits to be placed on this meddling done in the name of making us more sensitive?

Notable Sexual Harassment Penalties 2010–2011

Sexual harassment cases can be quite costly. The graphic depicts some of the larger settlements that resulted from sexual harassment charges filed with the US Equal Employment Opportunity Commission (EEOC) against the types of employers listed in 2010 and 2011.

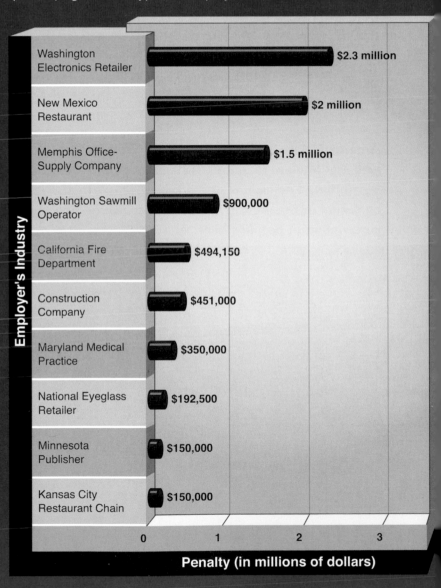

Employer's Industry

Industry	Penalty
Washington Electronics Retailer	$2.3 million
New Mexico Restaurant	$2 million
Memphis Office-Supply Company	$1.5 million
Washington Sawmill Operator	$900,000
California Fire Department	$494,150
Construction Company	$451,000
Maryland Medical Practice	$350,000
National Eyeglass Retailer	$192,500
Minnesota Publisher	$150,000
Kansas City Restaurant Chain	$150,000

Penalty (in millions of dollars)

Taken from: "The Costs of Sexual Harassment." J.J. Keller & Associates, Inc.," 2012. www.jjkeller.com/wcsstore /CVCatalogAssetStore/images/promotions/sh/Sexual–Harassment_J–J–Keller_infographic.pdf.

Note that I believe that instructors should reprimand students for grossly insulting their classmates. But it should not be the federal government's business to control conversation among students; nor do I see any reason for bureaucrats at the state level to perform this task. Moreover, the AAUW report makes reference to "negative remarks" that students are supposed to be making against gays. This reference seems so loaded that one has to wonder whether the accusers are seeking to punish people for disagreeing with their socially leftist views. Are Christian students or teachers who openly disapprove of gay relations engaging in "negative remarks"? In Canada such accusations have led to criminal charges being brought against

American Association of University Women (AAUW) lobbyists prepare to address US senators on sexual harassment legislation. The author says a recent report by the AAUW on sexual harassment is an attempt to overly involve the government in people's lives.

the "hate speaker" for being in violation of the federal human rights code.

It should also be clear that male adolescents behave differently from the female kinds (No, Virginia, gender identities are not entirely social constructs); and that flirting with and acting out before females is characteristic of males, and not only of the human ones. The feminists may try to change this by reducing us all to amoebas; but despite the recent successes of social engineering, embattled feminists may still have trouble totally eradicating male identity traits.

Lastly I would note that bringing suits against males for harassing speech often entails "hurtful interactions." An offended female, even one who decides long after the hurtful stare or unwelcome remarks that she is offended, can bring charges against the offending male. All she needs are a willing attorney (who may take the case on contingency), the appropriate legal form, and a judge who will hear her case. The young lady can then inflict lots of damage, financial and otherwise, on the defendant. Suits of this kind may earn the attorney between one-third and one-half of the settlement, and there is no scarcity of judges who will listen to such cases. Even if the plaintiff loses, her legal costs will be slight. It is private institutions and hapless individuals who have to protect themselves against such procedures; and private schools may be what the AAUW has its sights on.

Presumably public schools already enjoy the special attention of state and federal bureaucracies and teachers' unions; it is the private ones, and particularly religiously traditional ones, that are a tempting target for government-employed social manipulators. In such enclaves one can still encounter defenses of gender distinctions and critical remarks about the gay movement. Encouraging legal suits against such institutions, under Title Nine or whatever legal hook one finds for one's grievance, may be exactly what feminist activists have in mind.

SIX

Online Sexual Harassment Is a Serious Problem

Megan

Megan is a contributor to the activist website Hollaback!, which is dedicated to combating sexual harassment. In the following viewpoint Megan argues that sexual harassment, experienced as a daily reality by women throughout history, has become more invasive and intrusive in the digital age. She points out that being online has become centrally important to the lives of modern people, making them vulnerable to new forms of harassment. Techniques women have developed for dealing with harassment from strangers in public are ill suited for the new reality, where unwanted text, phone, or e-mail messages can invade private space at any time and in any place. Despite this, the police do not consider sexual harassment "real" unless a direct physical threat is present. Megan asserts that the problem needs to be taken more seriously because women have the right to feel safe in the digital world.

I recently had the painfully unpleasant (but all too common) experience of being sexually harassed by a man. I was harassed in a digital age, when creepy men can invade your personal space by sending their unwanted and invasive attention straight to you, regardless of where you are or what you are doing. I was sexually harassed while I was enjoying dinner at home with my family and friends, this creep's crass thoughts and words flooding me with fear and shame in the comfort of the home I grew up in. I was sexually harassed while I was working at school, this asshole's demented ideas trashing my consciousness and the innocent environment it was meant to be nourishing. I was sexually harassed and it was NOT OK. It IS not OK. But when I reported it to the local police force meant to protect me from this kind of creep—this ONE creep of an entire species of creeps pervading the male-world we live in—it informed me that this sexual harassment WAS, in fact, OK because it did not place me in any sort of direct existential danger, and that if he continued to harass me I should simply change my number and avoid the areas I typically see him creeping around.

When I hung up the phone with the police I thought to myself: Something here is terribly wrong.

The Changing Nature of Sexual Harassment

Now let us be frank about this endemic plague called sexual harassment that male homo sapiens can't seem to kick. It shares the same qualities of all of society's ugliest actualities, but is experienced by an entire gender group, worldwide, and everyday. To be female in the world—today, yesterday and tomorrows to come—is to be subject to sexual harassment by men. For women, sexual harassment is as pervasive and (dare I say) NATURAL an everyday part of our realities as breathing: it is in us and outside of us from our youth on up to adulthood, a period through which we develop our own personal means of dealing with it while trying to fulfill ourselves meaningfully in a world built up against us. I have historically dealt with it through silence, ignoring the presumptive "hey baby's" and "nice ass's" by quickening my pace and turning my face from the eyes and mouths violating me. A friend of mine plays crazy, staring blankly or yelling incoherently at her perpetrators' advances until they finally back off (needless to say, some don't). Yes, we women have our ways of dealing with the sick and unfair reality our sexist history has constructed for us, and to varying degrees they allow us to get through the day to day.

But today our methods, my methods especially, are dated. Today, my (admittedly) passive silent reaction to a man's harassment protects me from him about as much as a cigarette protects a smoker from getting lung cancer: Not only does my silence fail to protect me, it makes the situation worse. As I repeatedly erased the explicitly crude messages invading my phone and interrupting my life—my life as I was CHOOSING to experience it—I was giving this creep the power to manipulate my immediate condition and surroundings. When I simply closed out the digital garbage littering my laptop's inbox and polluting my mind, I was allowing this jerk the liberty to control how I was feeling and thinking at that time. And when I reported this unjust robbery of my self-determination, I was told that silence and avoidance would be the only means of coping with the harassment until it transpired into something more "real": a response which, rather than providing me a sense of comfort and consolation from fear, stirred in me a very deep sense of rage, and a firm new determination to never feel that fear again.

New Opportunities and New Dangers in the Digital World

We live in a world today where people die from the lives they lead in digital media. Kids commit suicide from cyber bullying, people are trafficked into fatal situations, and women get harassed—and abused, and prostituted, and raped and killed—in a cyberspace that increasingly takes on the oppressive patriarchal [ruled by men] qualities of the society that produced it. Not only do women now have the "real" male-oriented world to navigate and survive in, we also have the equivocally real, male-oriented cyber-reality to navigate and survive in, the latter's very "unreality" making it all the more dangerous. Who we women choose to participate [with] in our everyday "real" lives is something that is fortunately very much in our control, despite the abrasive harassment which inevitably invades them. We are free to pick and

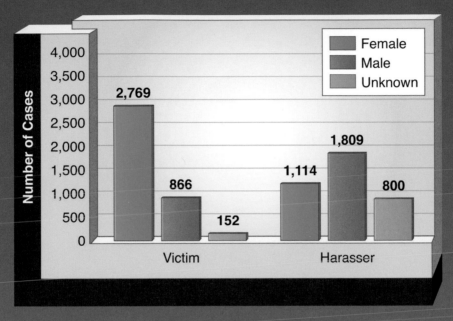

Gender of Victims and Perpetrators of Online Harassment, 2000–2012

Victim — Female: 2,769; Male: 866; Unknown: 152

Harasser — Female: 1,114; Male: 1,809; Unknown: 800

Taken from: "Online Harassment/Cyberstalking Statistics: Cumulative Statistics for the Years 2000–2012." WHO@ (Working to Halt Online Abuse), 2013. www.haltabuse.org/resources/stats/cumulative2000–2012.pdf.

choose what male attention we wish to fill those lives with, while surviving the grimy reality of unwanted male attention because we are women and that is what we women do. Who we invite to participate in our digitized lives, however, is something entirely different. While our digital livelihoods are not something we are completely powerless over, they do involve spaces that make our digital (and real) selves more readily accessible and vulnerable to unwanted attention, gazes and words. Creepy men will, and are, invading those spaces, and it is not something that will stop by simply ignoring it or keeping your mouth shut. Cigarettes will kill you. Silence will make this harassment worse. So consider this my own little vernacular vendetta against the creep who thought it was OK to f--- with me, to make me feel belittled, ashamed and afraid. . . . But it's more than that. It's a statement

Being online has become central to the lives of modern people, making them vulnerable to new forms of harassment.

that this kind of harassment is more pervasive and less tolerable in today's digital age than the former kind was, currently is, or ever will be in the future. It is ubiquitous and just as menacing, dangerous and unacceptable as any other form of harassment or abuse for the very real and tragic consequences we've seen it create. Why should a woman being sexually harassed on the street be given different consideration than one being sexually harassed in the privacy of her own home? Why must a woman feel the direct physical fear of a man for her fear to be taken seriously by the law, and why have our laws failed to acknowledge this fear manifesting itself in new forms, through our new medias and in our new digital selves?

Freedom from fear is not a right limited to the world we actively live in, but one that extends into the worlds we create with our language and means of expression. The fact that the digital worlds we populate are not real in a corporeal sense does not absolve us [from] the moral responsibility we have to endow those worlds with a bit of humanity. The fear I felt every day the aforementioned creep harassed me was unquestionably real, though that fear's source was "not." If fear can blur the lines separating our "real" selves from our digital selves and our "real" worlds from our digital worlds, freedom from fear can do it too, in a very loud way.

SEVEN

Mobile Online Technology Is Helping to Combat Sexual Harassment

Cassie Spodak

Cassie Spodak is a journalist in Washington, D.C. In the following viewpoint Spodak reports on how mobile technology is empowering people to fight back against sexual harassment. Hollaback!, an organization founded by Emily May and Oraia Reid, allows those who experience sexual harassment to report what happened using smartphone applications, or apps; the stories are then posted on the website on a global map. According to the founders, this makes the problem more visible to both regular citizens and lawmakers, as well as empowering users of the network by hearing stories of women effectively fighting back against harassment. In one inspirational case a video was posted online of Nicola Briggs confronting a man who harassed her on a train; by enlisting bystanders and alerting the authorities, she was able to have the man arrested. Briggs now writes for Hollaback!, helping to break the silence that often surrounds sexual harassment.

By now, everybody knows that mobile technology has transformed the way we share information.

Now a digital network called Hollaback! is using the latest tech to change the way victims and witnesses react to sexual harassment.

Hollaback!, which launched as an app [application] and website where victims of sexual abuse could report incidents, plans to launch a new app in March 2012 that will let bystanders report cases of sexual harassment as well.

The new network will be called "I've Got Your Back," and the group is currently raising money for the project through the crowd-funding site IndieGoGo. [The app is now available.]

Mapping Sexual Harassment Incidents

They plan to launch Android and iPhone apps, as well as an online map that aggregates reports from people who witness harassment.

The campaign was motivated out of a desire to "map something happy," said Emily May, co-founder and executive director of Hollaback!

"What 'happy' happens in the world of street harassment? What about when people intervene?" May told CNN.

Hollaback!'s previous efforts have focused on getting victims of sexual abuse to report crimes online.

The group began in 2005 as a blog run by a group of friends living in New York. Each member had come into contact with behavior on the streets of New York that made them feel victimized, and reporting harassment to the police didn't seem to help, they said.

The blog re-launched on the global platform iHollaback.org in September of 2010 and smartphone apps debuted in November [2010]. By allowing victims of street harassment to share their experiences, and even send pictures, the campaign quickly caught on internationally. Hollaback! now has blogs in 24 cities around the world, with 30 more set to launch in August [2011].

Sharing Experiences of Sexual Harassment

The website's aim is not to prosecute offenders.

"We don't advocate for fear mongering. We want to address the problem head on but in a way that is empowering," said Oraia Reid, co-founder of Hollaback!

The site's homepage displays a world map showing the different locations where individuals have experienced harassment. Visitors to the site can read about victims' experiences anywhere from New York City to Nigeria to China.

The founders see the mapping system as an effective way of reaching not just regular citizens, but also lawmakers who may be unaware of harassment in their communities. It also helps victims of street harassment realize that "the experience of street harassment is universal," said May.

"We're making change the same way it has always happened— by telling stories," she said. "We just have more tools to tell our stories now."

May told CNN that mobile technology has allowed the site to tap into a global community of activists. "Being able to tell those stories and visualize those stories in different ways has served as a catalyst," she said.

Many of these activists are young people searching for a way to be heard. May said 74% of the site's users are 29 or younger, 44% identify as gay, lesbian or transgendered and 26% identify as racial minorities, she said.

Confronting a Sexual Predator

Nicola Briggs' story illustrates the power that technology has to call attention to issues like sexual harassment. Briggs became a YouTube sensation when a video of her confronting a sexual predator on the subway went viral.

During rush hour on a downtown train in Manhattan last September [2010], Briggs felt a pressure on her back. When she tried to move away she still felt it. When she turned around she says she realized that a man behind her had been pressing his exposed genitals against her back.

New smartphone apps allow those who experience sexual harassment to post the incident on a global map on the Hollaback! website.

There are about 600 complaints of sex offenses in the New York subway system per year, according to the New York Police Department [NYPD].

James P. Hall, Chief of the Transit Bureau for the NYPD, said many of the crimes likely go unreported. Sexual harassment is the No. 1 quality of life concern in the subway in New York, he said.

Briggs, at 5-feet tall and with 17 years of self-defense training, said that it took her no time to react.

"I announced it to the entire train," she said. "He had special pants with no zipper. Everyone stopped talking on the train and then women starting screaming. Men started shouting."

Refusing to Be Silenced

Briggs told men in the train to guard the doors and she kept yelling at the man until transit police officers arrived and handcuffed

Hollaback! Map of Sexual Harassment Incidents in Halifax, Nova Scotia

Android and iPhone users around the world can download an app from Hollaback! that they can use to report sexual harassment incidents tagged by geographic location. The information gathered is displayed on online maps. The visual depicts a map of Halifax, Nova Scotia, Canada, on April 2, 2013. Visitors to the sites (available for many different locations around the world) can click on the place markers to get more information about specific sexual harassment incidents.

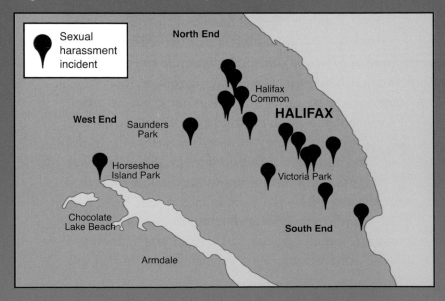

him. She told CNN that one man threatened to punch the perpetrator in the face if he tried to escape.

The man harassing Briggs was sentenced to four months in jail. An illegal immigrant, he was deported to Mexico in February [2011], according to officials.

In Briggs' case the role of the bystanders was essential, she said.

"When someone is in need you have to step up and put aside your own needs," she told CNN.

Hollaback! contacted Briggs after the video became public and she now regularly posts on the website about her experiences and feelings on street harassment.

"You have to be willing to call up your reserves and say, 'Can someone help me?' This shouldn't happen to me or anyone else," said Briggs. "It will go away. It's only when you feel shameful that he wins. He silenced you in that moment, he silenced you later."

But Briggs sees Hollaback! as a way to break this silence.

"With Hollaback! you see what you say can totally turn it around."

EIGHT

Public Sexual Harassment ("Street Harassment") Is a Serious Problem That Requires Legal Regulation

Holly Kearl

Holly Kearl runs the website Stop Street Harassment and a companion blog where people from around the world submit their street harassment stories. She also authored *Stop Street Harassment: Making Public Places Safe and Welcoming for Women.* In the following viewpoint Kearl cites statistics showing that street harassment is a very common experience for women. Her own research reveals that such experiences, which can range from sexual comments to assault, make women more afraid of public spaces and limits their freedom. Kearl notes that it has been illegal to sexually harass women at work since 1964, and she suggests that it is time to make street harassment illegal as well. More important, a shift in cultural attitude is needed so that people no longer consider any form of sexual harassment tolerable. Legal regulation, Kearl believes, will help lead to this needed change in public perception.

Do you remember when it was legal for a man to make sexually explicit or sexist remarks to a woman at work? I don't. While sexual harassment in the workplace still happens, it became illegal under Title VII of the Civil Rights Act of 1964, 19 years before I was born.

Do you remember when it was legal for a man to make sexually explicit or sexist remarks to a woman on the street or at a bus stop? I do. Sexual harassment in public is legal. But it shouldn't be.

Sexual harassment in public, often called street harassment, is a real problem that requires legal regulation. It ranges from legal acts like leering, whistling, honking, sexual comments, sexist comments, and following, to illegal acts like groping, public masturbation, and

Members of the group Hollaback! rally in Washington, D.C., in support of legislation to protect women from street harassment.

assault. While some might argue that street harassment isn't a common occurrence, in actuality, most American women have experienced it in some form. In an Indiana University, Indianapolis, study conducted in the early 1990s, 100 percent of the 293 women interviewed could cite multiple incidents of street harassment. Similarly, 100 percent of the 54 women interviewed in the California Bay Area in the early 2000s for a Northwestern University study had been the target of offensive or sexually suggestive remarks on multiple occasions. In 2007, the Manhattan Borough President's Office surveyed 1,790 transit riders in New York City [NYC] and found that 63 percent had been sexually harassed on the subway.

Street Harassment Leads to Fear of Public Spaces

Adding to the limited research on the topic are hundreds of street harassment stories women share on blogs like HollaBack NYC and Stop Street Harassment. And I bet if you ask, most women you know will be able to cite at least a few times they have been harassed.

The threat or experience of street harassment, often combined with a socialization to be fearful of male-perpetrated sexual assault in public, means women tend to be more wary of public places than men. The resulting impact on their lives is stunning, as I found when I informally surveyed more than 800 women from 23 countries in 2008 for a forthcoming book [*Stop Street Harassment*, published in 2010]. Sixty percent of women said they "always" constantly assess their surroundings. Eighty percent said that at least some times they avoid being in public alone. Eighteen percent said actual or feared interactions with strangers impacted their decision to move from their neighborhood. The more often a woman reported being harassed—or if a man had assaulted her—the more likely it was that she practiced several strategies that restricted her freedom.

Women will never achieve equality with men until they have equal access to public places and the resources and opportunities they hold. And it seems women never will have equal access to public places until men stop harassing and assaulting them there.

What can we do?

© Mashanda Lazarus

I suggest we look to Egypt for guidance. In January [2010], groundbreaking legislation banning sexual harassment at work, in public, online, and through mobile devices was introduced in the Egyptian Parliament. Last month [February 2010] the legislation moved to Parliament's legislative affairs committee. The pending legislation is indicative of an important cultural shift occurring in Egypt that I'd like to see happen in the United States.

A Cultural Shift Is Needed

The shift started in earnest in 2008, when the Egyptian Centre for Women's Rights (ECWR) surveyed over 2,000 women and men throughout Egypt about public sexual harassment. Their findings were not dissimilar from studies conducted in the United States. More than 83 percent of women said men had harassed them in public and more than 60 percent of men readily admitted to harassing women.

The report and related efforts of the ECWR has propelled change across Egypt since 2008. Women's enrollment in self-defense classes shot up. Women began using an audio blogging station, Banat wa Bas, to share their harassment stories and vent their frustrations. *Kelmetna*, a magazine for youth, launched a campaign called "Respect yourself: Egypt still has real men" with weekly seminars, self defense classes, and street concerts. There are more than 53,000 members of their Facebook group.

And now, under pressure from activists, it is likely the Egyptian government will pass legislation making sexual harassment in public illegal.

The United States needs a similar cultural shift regarding street harassment. Street harassment is not a joke about construction workers; it is a problem that touches every woman's life at some level and prevents women on a whole from achieving equality. More research needs to be conducted to better track its prevalence and to uncover the root causes, and in the meantime, let's make it illegal. While laws do not solve problems, they can help change social attitudes, deter the undesired behavior, and provide affected persons with options for recourse.

You and I remember when sexual harassment in public was legal, but I hope the next generation will not.

NINE

Women Need to Confront Sexual Harassers

Katie J.M. Baker

Katie J.M. Baker writes for the feminist website Jezebel. In the following viewpoint Baker argues that men have been taught to view sexually harassing behaviors such as "catcalling" as harmless, but that women who are targeted feel threatened and intimidated. According to the author, men do not realize what it is like to live with the constant threat of rape or to feel that one is always being evaluated and judged on the basis of sexual attractiveness. Baker says men are taught by the behavior of other men, as well as by women's silence, to erroneously view harassment as "a fun, inoffensive social activity." She suggests that women need to talk back to harassers in order to teach men that it is not acceptable to sexually harass women. She says that when she explained to men on the street how their comments felt to her, many of them apologized for their bad behavior.

*H*ey, *sexy mama! How'd you get so fine?*
Jesus, look at those legs.

I'm used to ignoring the terms of endearment yelled at me by strange men on the street. Like most women I know, I treat street harassment like unpleasant weather—a common occurrence I silently endure by drawing my coat tighter around my body and walking briskly ahead with a stiff neck. But . . . I'd been promising myself I'd take the plunge for weeks, and on this particular day I finally snapped.

"I want to know why you think it's OK to talk to me like that," I heard my five-foot-two, small-boned self saying in a voice I wished was less shaky.

"I just appreciate a beautiful woman," the man said back with a smile.

"OK," I said, "if you appreciate me, you can tell me I'm beautiful in a respectful way. But you're treating me like I'm not a human being. No woman likes that, and it doesn't make me feel beautiful."

The man looked confused. "I'm really, really sorry," he said. "I have sisters, and I understand where you're coming from."

Sexual Harassment Feels Threatening

After a few more seemingly genuine apologies I walked away. I was pleased, slightly cynical (could I really have gotten through to this man in less than 30 seconds?), but most of all shocked that this was my first time talking back to a street harasser. I consider myself a feminist, and am widely known as someone who's never afraid to speak her mind. Why, then, am I inherently hard-wired to ignore every whistle, lip smack, or holler?

Some men may wonder why I care so much, why I let street harassment get to me. Maybe you think I'm overreacting by lecturing strangers who only want to compliment me, after all. "I'd be thrilled if a woman on the street told me I was sexy," a male friend once said to me after I expressed my frustration.

I'm happy to address those questions (and will, later on)—and I understand that it can be difficult to understand how threatening a seemingly harmless "Smile, beautiful!" can feel—but let's get one thing straight. Go ask any woman in your life whom you respect—mother, sister, cousin, lover, or friend—how it makes her feel when she's loudly and publicly objectified, the recipient of obscene comments like "suck my %*#&," or followed down the street. I promise you that it doesn't make her feel good or beautiful or respected.

People Need to Talk Back to Sexual Harassers

Street harassment has a negative effect on us all. No single man wants the actions of a few to be attributed to his entire gender, but studies show that male harassers impact victims' perception and reaction to men in general. Still, most street harassers aren't "bad men"—they don't fully realize why their actions are hurtful or disrespectful to the female population. Sometimes they don't even realize they are harassing women at all.

That's why it won't end until both men and women start engaging with harassers.

New York City lawmakers are considering an official catcalling ban, but I'm not sure how successful that could be. Is it really possible to prevent people from talking or calling out to others on the street? More importantly, do we want it to be? While passive objectification can be just as hurtful as the aggressive kind, monitoring it can be much more complicated.

Hollaback!, a group "dedicated to ending street harassment using mobile technology," encourages women to, well, "holla back" by sharing stories and photos using social media. Hollaback! is a wonderful movement, and definitely a step in the right direction in terms of drawing attention to the cause. But it can only be so effective when the harasser has no idea he's being "hollered back" at.

Responding Assertively Feels Empowering

I believe reacting online is an approach too detached to make a significant impact. The more I safely challenge my harassers—and see how they almost always step down—the more I realize that we can't depend on lawmakers or our cell phones to do all of the work for us. So I have a radical idea: Instead of thinking of all street harassers solely as criminals who deserve penalization and public ridicule, we need to communicate with them about how it feels to be the target of their actions.

I know some will be angry with me (hi, Mom) for proposing what may seem like a dangerous idea. Confronting street harassers is not always possible in every situation or for everyone. To be sure, it's a very bad idea to engage with those who have truly harmful intentions, and if even a small part of you feels threatened, you should walk away.

But (according to Hollaback!, interestingly enough) studies show that those who "respond assertively" to harassment are less vulnerable. It's possible—if your harasser or leerer seems more ignorant than dangerous, and you're in a well-lit area with people nearby—to succinctly and calmly explain why certain actions are disrespectful.

The First Recorded Case of Sexual Harassment

I want to challenge all good men to step up. Men, please say something when you witness street harassment, even if the harassers are your coworkers or friends. I'm not saying all men are responsible for their street harassing ilk, but they owe it to the women they respect to set an example and encourage others to do the same.

In Plautus' *Mercator*, written around 200 BC, Demipho turns away the beautiful slave girl bought for his mother by his son Charinus. "She is hardly the proper sort of person," says Demipho. "Why not?" asks Charinus (who is secretly in love with the girl, as is—naturally—his father). "Because it would cause scandal if such a beauty were the attendant of a wife and mother," Demipho replies. "When she passes through the streets all the men would look at her, leer, nod and wink and whistle."

This is the first known recording of a form of bullying that, thousands of years later, the vast majority of women experience on a regular basis. Today it has evolved into a variety of behaviors, often arranged by severity from physical contact and verbal abuse to stares and whistles. Other forms include exposing, picture-taking, groping, masturbating, threatening, intimidating, stalking, and attention-seeking behavior like flattering and honking.

Sexual Harassment as a Form of Male Bonding

As a woman, I've experienced almost all of these variations more than once. There's no doubt that some street harassers are more

The author contends that women must confront males who they believe are sexually harassing them so that the men become aware of their behavior and how it affects others.

dangerous than others; gropers, for example, trump picture-takers any day. But I'm not as interested in discussing why rapists, stalkers, or "flashers" do what they do. I'm more intrigued by the watchers and callers.

In Beth A. Quinn's workplace-focused study, "Sexual Harassment and Masculinity: The Power and Meaning of 'Girl Watching'" she notes that "no man discussed girl watching in initial accounts of his workplace."

[She adds,] "I suspect that they did not consider it to be relevant to a discussion of their average workday, even though it became apparent that it was an integral daily activity for some groups of men."

It not only shows how second-nature street harassment is to some men—hello, it's been going on since at least 200 BC—but how it often isn't about the interchangeable female targets as much as it is about male bonding, defining one's own masculinity, or collectively—even if subconsciously—asserting men's inherent physical power over women.

The Revealing Origins of Slang Terms

"As embarrassing as this is to admit, I feel like the main reason my friends and I objectify women is to let each other know that we're straight," a male friend of mine told me. Later, a man I confronted on the street told me I was his "dream girl" and asked me to let him prove himself to me in more obscene terms. "This is just what guys do," he said. "We're just joking around. No offense!"

Let's take a look at the etymological origins of the most common slang terms for street harassment. While "wolf-whistle" does have a predatory connotation—wolves have been symbols of male lust since the Elizabethan era, and the specific use of wolf for "sexually aggressive male" was first recorded in the mid-1800s—most other terms are more similar to "girl watching" in the sense that they are not as much aggressive as they are critical or male-exclusive.

For example, the first documented "catcallers" were theatergoers in the 1700s who whistled and jeered to express disapproval for actors or actions onstage. It wasn't until the 20th century that the word took on a sexual meaning, but the basic idea is the same: the catcaller's right to vocally judge the catcallee. He's an audience member expected to give feedback to a performance.

Men Are Taught to Think Harassment Is Harmless

"Hubba hubba" caught on during World War II when Marine Harry H. Miller used the phrase—commonly used at his military camp to mean "double time" or "hurry up"—to draw his friend's attention to a group of beautiful women, using a term "he knew only his buddy would understand."

Catcallers and hubba-hubba-ers aren't, for the most part, women-haters. They catcall because they're taught by their elders, peers, and effectively by the women that ignore them that street harassment is a fun, inoffensive social activity. For centuries, more or less well meaning men have gleaned that it's acceptable, even funny.

Am I saying men should never talk to women in public? No, not at all.

How to Talk Respectfully to Women in Public

There's a huge difference between harassing a woman and trying to start a conversation. Here are some tips: talk to her, not at her. Treat her with respect: be aware of her personal space, ask her how she's doing or what she's reading instead of commenting on her body parts, look at her face instead of her chest. If she ignores you, drops eye contact, or walks away, back off. It wasn't rude of you to approach her, but she's not being rude if she doesn't want to keep talking to you, especially if you initiated conversation while she was running an errand, waiting for the bus, or on her computer at a coffee shop.

Let's say you're not interested in having an actual conversation, but just want to let a woman know she's beautiful. Go ahead, it's a free country; just do it respectfully. Don't be threatening, don't make animal sounds, don't follow her. Most women I know wouldn't be offended if someone told her she was looking great or had gorgeous hair or a beautiful smile. But don't expect the woman in question to feel the same way, and don't act aggressive if she rejects your advances.

Studies suggest that 80 to 100 percent of all women face at least occasional unwanted, harassing attention in public places from men they do not know.

The Constant Threat of Rape

Many men (like my friend, quoted above) insist they'd be "thrilled" to be shouted at on the street. So why don't women feel flattered? Because we live with the threat of rape—the knowledge that one in every six American women will be sexually assaulted in her lifetime. Even if a man has "innocent" intentions when he yells "Hey sexy!" at a woman, he has a good chance of making her feel

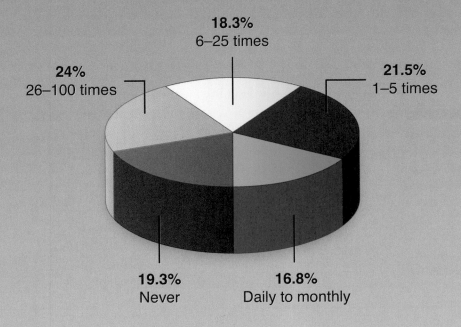

How Often Women Experience Strangers Making Sexually Explicit Comments to Them

18.3%
6–25 times

24%
26–100 times

21.5%
1–5 times

19.3%
Never

16.8%
Daily to monthly

Taken from: Holly Kearl. "Always on Guard: Women and Street Harassment." *AAUW Outlook*, Spring 2009. www.hollykearl.com/writing/.

uncomfortable, angry, or frightened. She's likely to automatically connect the moment with other negative street harassment experiences she's had—or, worse, with memories of more serious assault.

When a woman catcalls a man, it's far more likely to be considered "charming" or "flattering" because there's usually no chance that the woman could force the man into a dangerous situation by sheer physical force or intimidation.

Men: would you find it complimentary if it were commonplace for other men to yell out "I'd like to take that home with me" or "Why the sad face? I'll give you something to smile about" while following you down the street? Men who could, hypothetically, force you to go home with them if they wanted? Think about it. I suspect most of you would feel uncomfortable, threatened, even scared.

More Subtle Forms of Harassment

What about the most passive of street harassers, the ones who don't say anything outwardly insulting or objectifying—or maybe don't say anything at all? They're harder to confront without feeling like an asshole. I had a cold last week, and one morning stumbled and sneezed my way to the supermarket in pajamas and a messy bun to get some soup. I was reaching for the Campbells when I turned around and nearly bumped into a man who was standing less than an inch away from me, staring at me intently. "You are so beautiful," he said, feet firmly planted in my personal space. "Why aren't you smiling?" I had to literally step around him and make my way down another aisle before he stopped leering at me.

Afterward, I was furious—not just because of the way that man made me feel, but because I'm honestly unsure if it's OK to feel such anger in similar situations. The man didn't say anything objectifying, make any animal sounds, or gesture at me inappropriately. But even if he didn't catcall me, so to speak, he made me feel like I was on stage—and, especially in my sniffling state (and trust me, although this is somewhat irrelevant, I did not look my best), I was resentful that I was made to feel intimidated when all I wanted was a can of soup.

Plus, why should I have to smile? In a post expressing her own frustration with being hit on while running errands, blogger Almie Rose laments that "as women, we're subliminally taught to be polite under duress. Because if we say no, or reject any sort of advance even if we do it kindly, we're labeled a bitch." It's true: many women I know say a "smile, beautiful!" frustrates them more than an obscene come-on. It all comes back to the same point: women aren't performing for you.

What about the women, like "Subway Badass" Nicola Briggs, who respond creatively to street harassers? Briggs became a folk hero for frustrated women everywhere when a video of her yelling at a guy for "flashing" her on the subway recently went viral. In 2008, an Israeli tourist became so fed up with construction-worker catcallers while visiting New Zealand that she actually stripped in front of them in exasperation.

Respect and Personal Boundaries

Frustratingly, society tends to punish, not congratulate, those who speak up. Briggs hated the fact that TV stations blurred her face when airing her video—it gave "the wrong message to women" by making her into a victim instead of a victor. The Israeli woman was similarly victim-shamed when told by police that her behavior was "inappropriate"—"She's not an unattractive looking lady," one policeman told the press—while her catcallers probably enjoyed the best workday of their lives.

The bottom line is to treat others with respect. If you approach a woman, be aware of her personal boundaries and talk to her as if she is a person, not a sex object. If she's clearly disinterested, know when to back away. And, for God's sake, don't whistle. She is not a farm animal.

I'm loath to say that respect works both ways in these situations—it's hard to treat street harassers kindly. (If I were confronted by someone who clearly has serious issues—like Briggs' flasher—I'd go ahead and yell my head off.) But I've personally found that speaking calmly and clearly is more constructive than yelling (which, trust me, I've also done).

These days, when I'm harassed and feel that I'm in a safe enough situation to communicate with my harasser, I think about Plautus' slave girl. I remember that I have just as much a right to go about my day without being harassed as does anyone else. And I remember that unless I do engage, nothing will change. Should we have to explain why "I'd like a piece of that" is demeaning? No—but if we make a habit of it, fewer will need the lesson.

TEN

Men Need to Take an Active Role in Ending Sexual Harassment

Michael Flood

> Michael Flood is a lecturer in sociology at the University of Wollongong in Australia. His research interests include prevention of violence against women, men and gender, male heterosexuality, and sexual and reproductive health. In the following viewpoint Flood argues that although most men do not engage in sexual harassment, the majority of those who do harass are male, and the majority of those who are the targets of harassment are female. Although most men do not approve of sexual harassment, typically they remain silent or ignore such behaviors when they occur. According to the author, good men have an important role to play in preventing harassment, by actively setting a good example by treating women with respect and speaking out when they see other men treating women disrespectfully.

Sexual harassment will only disappear when men take an active role in ending it. Most men don't harass, and most don't condone it. But sexual harassment is largely a problem of men's behaviour, against women and other men. Four of every five harassers are male, according to a recent national survey. Two thirds of incidents involve a male harasser and female target, and another fifth involve male harassers and male targets.

Most men think sexual harassment is unacceptable. But too often we turn a blind eye, stay silent, or laugh along, if only to cover our own embarassment. And too many senior male leaders have offered token platitudes rather than real action.

I support the White Ribbon Campaign, which focuses on the positive roles men can play in preventing men's violence against women. The campaign recognises that this violence—whether harassment, domestic violence, or rape—is a 'men's issue'. It harms the women and girls we love, gives all men a bad name, and is perpetrated by men we know. A minority of men treat women with contempt, and it is up to the majority of men to help create a culture in which this is unthinkable.

Men march in the White Ribbon Campaign's Walk a Mile in Her Shoes rally to raise public awareness of sexual harassment issues.

Attitudes Toward Rape and Sexual Assault Jokes

Some people believe that US culture is a "rape culture" that discounts the seriousness of sexual harassment and assault, thereby increasing the likelihood of such violations. An *Oklahoma Daily* poll found respondents evenly divided on whether humor about sexual assault is acceptable, while a *60 Minutes/Vanity Fair* poll found more men than women believe such humor is never acceptable.

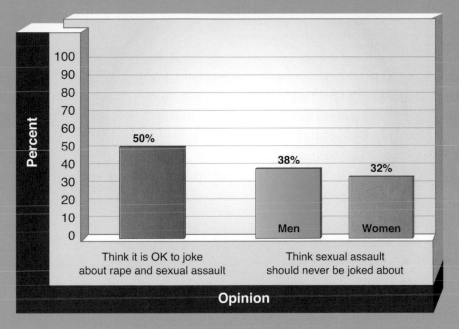

Taken from: "EDITORIAL: When You Joke About Rape You Protect, Enable Rapists," *Oklahoma Daily*, February 8, 2012. www.oudaily.com/news/2012/feb/08/editorial–when–you–joke–about–rape–you–are–technic/; "The *60 Minutes/Vanity Fair* Poll: Lust for Life," *Vanity Fair*, December 3, 2012. www.vanityfair.com/magazine/2013/01/poll–judd–apatow–comedy –issue#slide=3_slideshow_item2–3.

Set a Good Example: Speak Out

Men's sexual harassment of women often reflects sexist social norms [patterns of expected behavior] and gender inequalities in power. It is part of a continuum of abusive and coercive behaviours, including sexual violence.

Ending sexual harassment will mean shifting entrenched cultures of sexism and chauvinistic bonding in which women endure a daily 'dripping tap' of unwelcome sexual behaviour. It will mean tackling the homophobic abuse, bullying, and violent initiations involved in men's harassment of other men.

Men of goodwill can play a key role. Treat women with respect. Challenge peers who practise or condone harassment. Speak up when mates are making jokes or comments supportive of harassment and abuse. And support victims, female or male.

Leadership from men at the top is critical. Senior male leaders must become committed advocates for reforms to build respectful workplace cultures.

We'll also need education campaigns to undermine the dodgy gender norms which feed sexual harassment of women: women are sexual objects and men are women's superiors. Men are less likely than women to perceive incidents as harassment and more tolerant of harassing behaviour, particularly if they have traditional attitudes to gender.

Women have led the way in challenging sexual harassment. It's time for men to step up and join them.

ELEVEN

Abuse of Power: An Increase in Male-on-Male Sexual Harassment Shows Larger Truths About Abuse in the Workplace

Krista Gesaman

Krista Gesaman is a writer for the *Daily Beast*, a news and commentary website. In the following viewpoint the author reports that cases of sexual harassment of men have been on the rise in recent years. Gesaman claims that although there have been some cases of women harassing men, most of the cases involve male-on-male harassment. She says the increase might be due to male victims feeling more empowered to assert their rights, rather than an actual increase in incidents, noting that same-sex sexual harassment was not legally recognized until 1998. According to the author, sexual harassment increases when those in power feel threatened, which may be a factor in the current tough economic times. Another possible motivation is the desire to undermine coworkers by creating a hostile work environment to adversely affect their job performance.

The Cheesecake Factory is known for its oversize portions, delectable desserts, and family-friendly atmosphere. The restaurant is also accused of creating nothing but disturbing memories for a few of its employees. In 2008 the Equal Employment Opportunity Commission (EEOC) filed suit after six Cheesecake Factory staffers claimed they were subjected to repeated sexual harassment at the chain's Chandler Mall location in Phoenix, including allegations of sexual fondling, simulated rape, and even being physically dragged into the restaurant's refrigerator. The Cheesecake Factory denies the charges; in November the company settled the dispute by paying $340,000 to the victims.

Surprisingly, it wasn't a group of female workers who were compensated by the popular eatery: it was a group of male employees who claim they were sexually harassed by other men in the workplace. And, as new EEOC filings show, this situation is not unusual. Between 1992 and 2008, the percentage of sexual-harassment charges filed by men with the EEOC doubled from 8 percent to 16 percent. "While some people may think sexual harassment of male employees is a joke, the issue is real," says David Grinberg, spokesperson for the EEOC. "We are seeing more of it, and such conduct has serious legal consequences for employers."

There are instances when women sexually harass men, but the increase is due mainly to reports of men harassing other men, also called same-sex sexual harassment, Grinberg says. The EEOC tracks the number of men and women who file claims with the agency, but doesn't always keep track of the gender of the harasser. However, Grinberg confirms that the EEOC has recognized a growing trend in the number of men alleging same-sex sexual harassment.

"The classic image of sexual harassment is Clarence Thomas and Anita Hill; it's not two men or even two women," says Dr. Liza H. Gold, a clinical professor of psychiatry at Georgetown University who serves as an expert in sexual-harassment suits. And yet the experience of men harassed by men may help to illustrate the realities of all such cases. When women are the victims, they may face assumptions that the abuse is the result of an affair gone wrong, hurt feelings, or mixed signals. In truth, sexual harassment of both genders has more to do

In 2008 the Equal Employment Opportunity Commission (EEOC) filed suit after six Cheesecake Factory staffers claimed they were subjected to ongoing sexual harassment by other employees.

with issues of control and abuses of power for the purpose of humiliation than with sexual attraction.

By exposing the men to taunts about their genitalia, sexually suggestive simulations, and lewd comments, the men perpetrating the harassment are seeking to embarrass and target the male victims—not sexually stimulate or "flirt" with them. "Sexual harassment is about using power in a way to hurt somebody," says Marcia McCormick, associate professor at Saint Louis University School of Law, who specializes in employment law and gender issues. In the Cheesecake Factory suit there were no allegations that supervisors were attracted to the other men—the sexual harassment was a form of intimidation, McCormick says.

Same-sex harassment has been recognized by the courts for only a little more than 20 years. In 1998 the U.S. Supreme Court held in *Oncale v. Sundowner Offshore Services* that an individual can bring a claim for workplace harassment when the harasser and the harassed employee are the same sex. Joseph Oncale was working on an oil platform when he was sexually assaulted by three co-workers, one being a supervisor. What started as humiliating verbal attacks soon grew to physical violence, and on one occasion, Oncale was sodomized with a bar of soap. He quit soon after. Oncale may have been targeted because of his small stature—he was the shortest guy on the rig, and therefore an easy target—but those perpetrating sexual harassment can have a variety of motivations or triggers. "It's really hard to say what motivates someone to harass except a desire to humiliate the person being harassed," McCormick says.

Tough economic times have also been known to foster an environment of increased sexual harassment, says human-resources consultant Michele Paludi. Harassment escalates when those in power feel threatened, either by an influx of women workers or a challenge to the traditional gender expectations. It's possible that in an economic recession, more men feel powerless and fear for their job security, causing them to lash out at anyone perceived as a threat. "By creating a hostile work environment co-workers might miss deadlines or get negative performance reviews. The harasser might just be thinking, 'Better them than me,'" she says. The lack of financial resources could also mean that fewer supervisors or managers are trained to resolve sexual-harassment issues at work. "When there are hard times, there are certain programs in the workplace that are cut. We often see the training programs on sexual harassment

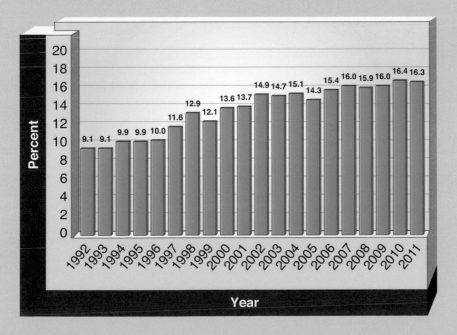

Percentage of Sexual Harassment Charges Filed by Males, 1992–2011

From 1992 to 2011 the percentage of sexual harassment charges filed by males through the US Equal Employment Opportunity Commission (EEOC) and Fair Employment Practice Agencies (FEPAs) has almost doubled.

Taken from: "Sexual Harassment Charges EEOC & FEPAs Combined: FY1992–FY1996 & FY1997–FY2011."
US Equal Employment Opportunity Commission. www.eeoc.gov/eeoc/statistics/enforcement/sexual_harassment
–a.cfm; www.eeoc.gov/eeoc/statistics/enforcement/sexual_harassment.cfm.

are cut completely or not offered once a year like they should be," Paludi adds.

It's also possible that same-sex harassment is not on the rise, but that male victims feel more empowered about reporting abuse. "People feel they can stand up and say, 'Hey you've violated my civil rights,'" Gold says. "They feel freer to pursue what 20 years ago would be considered a gender boundary."

TWELVE

Women Dressing Provocatively Does Not Contribute to Sexual Harassment

Hugo Schwyzer

Hugo Schwyzer is an author and speaker who has taught history and gender studies at Pasadena City College in California since 1993. He has presented workshops on sexual harassment, and he blogs at www.hugoschwyzer. net. In the following viewpoint Schwyzer argues that men are quite capable of controlling their sexual behavior, regardless of how provocatively some women choose to dress in public. He refutes claims by some men's rights advocates that women who wear revealing clothing in public are sexually harassing men by arousing desire in them without intending to actually have sex. According to the author, the real problem is that some men feel entitled to sexual gratification from women; however, sexual rejection is a fact of life that one must learn to accept. That a man feels sexually aroused by a woman does not in any way obligate her to fulfill that desire or to change her behavior to prevent his arousal.

One of the seemingly endless variations on the "men today are in crisis and it's mostly women's fault" trope [figure of speech] is the idea that most straight guys are completely incapable of figuring out what the other sex actually wants. Pop psychologists assure us that men are evolutionarily hardwired towards promiscuity, simplicity, and the inability to pick up on subtle clues. As a result, the theory holds, men are both easily manipulated and vulnerable to chronic misinterpretation of women's dress and behavior. So vulnerable, in fact, that some advocates for men are calling for a change in sexual harassment law: a change that would force women either to cover up—or put out. This, obviously, is bullshit, but the rationale behind it is even more ridiculous.

The latest iteration of this argument has the Antipodes [Australia and New Zealand] a-buzzing. Bettina Arndt argued in the *Sydney Morning Herald* [on February 11, 2012,] that "everywhere you look, women are stepping out dressed provocatively, but bristling if the wrong man shows he enjoys the display." (Remember, it's summer down under.) Arndt writes:

> [Men] are in a total state of confusion . . . Sensitive males are wary, not knowing where to look. Afraid of causing offense. And there are angry men, the beta males who lack the looks, the trappings of success to tick these women's boxes. They know the goodies on display are not for them. These are the men most likely to behave badly, blatantly leering, grabbing and sneering. For them, the whole thing is a tease. They know it and resent it.

Men Can, and Should, Control Their Sexual Behavior

There's nothing new about arguing that scantily-clad women drive helpless men to distraction—or worse. SlutWalkers [members of an organization protesting the blaming of a woman's appearance as the cause of rape] and Talmudic scholars (among others) have made the case over and over that nothing a woman wears (or doesn't wear) can cause a man to rape her, but their voices are

Percentage of Women Who Have Experienced Street Harassment

Most women around the world experience street harassment, whether in countries such as Egypt and Yemen, where clothing styles are very unrevealing, or in California's San Francisco Bay Area, where women often wear more revealing clothing.

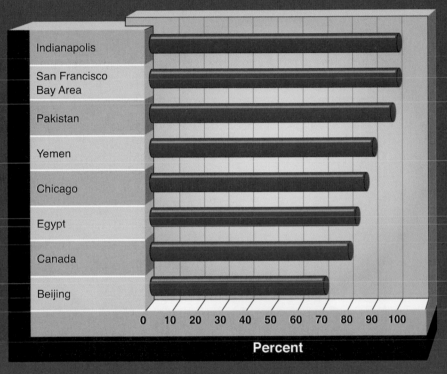

Taken from: "STATISTICS: 1—Nineteen Academic & Community Studies." Stop Street Harassment. www.stopstreetharassment.org/resources/statistics/.

often drowned out by those who ridiculously insist on outsourcing all male sexual self-control to women.

In Arndt's case, she goes beyond merely holding women responsible for their own rapes. Her op-ed implies that women who don't cover up are committing *an act of cruelty* against most men, most of the time. Arndt claims that a conventionally attractive woman who shows off her cleavage "is advertising her wares to the world, not just her target audience, and somehow men are expected to know when they are not on her page . . . But as we all know, many men are lousy at that stuff—the language totally escapes them."

Arndt's appeal to the universal "knowledge" of men's cluelessness is as casual as it is clumsy. She's right in the sense that our culture raises men to inadvertently confuse a woman's bare skin (or

The author maintains that men are quite capable of controlling their behavior, regardless of how provocatively some women choose to dress in public.

a smile, or direct eye contact) with a sexual come-on. But most men are not biologically incapable of either empathy or intuition. They can learn to distinguish sexual interest from politeness, a fashion choice from an attempt at seduction. Rejection from women (and "correction" from other men) is often how they learn.

Provocative Dress Does Not Create a "Hostile Environment"

Arndt doesn't believe men are capable of learning these non-verbal skills. More importantly, like many in the men's rights movement to which she's sympathetic, she doesn't think they should have to. She approvingly cites Rob Tiller, an Australian psychotherapist and men's advocate who refers to women who wear revealing clothing as committing "biological sexual harassment." This idea that women who go around "flaunting their bodies" are harassing men has become a pet issue for many in the North American men's rights movement. One site claims: "In many offices across America, women dress provocatively, showing inappropriate thigh and cleavage. This, in itself, is sexual harassment against men—but women get away with it, and men rarely complain."

Sexual harassment, of course, takes many forms. Tiller and his fellow men's rights activists (MRAs) seem to think that scantily-clad women are guilty of creating a "hostile environment." The term is the same in both Australian and American sexual harassment law, and refers to a workplace or school culture that tolerates unwanted sexual behavior. The law rejects the idea that a low-cut blouse or a short skirt might constitute a hostile environment, but that hasn't stopped the MRAs—or their allies like Arndt—from arguing that perhaps the law should be changed to recognize the damage that sexually tantalizing dress does to men.

The traditional arguments for women's modesty have been that concealing dress was necessary to protect men from lustful thoughts and to protect women from being raped. But Arndt and the MRAs have a different rationale. They're not offended by skimpy clothing on religious grounds, nor do they all buy into the myth of male weakness that says that bare female skin invariably causes otherwise nice guys to commit sexual assault. Rather, they seem to be arguing that by tempting *all* straight men while only being willing to sleep with a few, flirtatious or scantily-clad women are engaged in a particularly cruel form of sexualized discrimination. That, the MRAs insist, ought to be seen as sexual harassment.

Sexual Rejection Is a Fact of Life

For Arndt and her ideological fellow travelers, it's sexually unsuccessful straight men ("betas") that suffer the most from a culture in which women are free to display their bodies. Asking women to cover up isn't about protecting purity; for the MRAs it's about protecting betas from humiliation and from self-esteem-destroying reminders that they can look but never touch the bodies for which they long. All of that pent-up male resentment is women's fault, Arndt implies, and it is women's responsibility to consider the soul-scarring cost of the mixed messages their revealing clothing sends.

The kind of particularly male pain that Arndt and her allies describe isn't rooted in women's flirtatiousness, sexy clothing, or presumed preference for "alpha" males. Whether they're genuinely hurting or just petulantly sulking, the confusion and hurt with which men cope is based largely on their own sense of entitlement. The calculus of entitlement works like this: if women don't want to turn men on, they need to cover up. If they don't cover up, they'll turn men on. If they turn men on, women are obligated to do something to assuage that lust. Having turned them on, if women don't give men what they want, then women are cruel teases who have no right to complain if men lash out in justified rage at being denied what they've been taught is rightfully theirs.

The reality is that sexual rejection happens to men and women alike. That's part of living in a world in which for a host of reasons, we are not all equally attractive, and where the people we want to sleep with will not always want to sleep with us. The hard truth men and women alike need to grasp is a simple one: our arousal is not someone else's problem to solve. The sooner we encourage men in particular to grasp that truth, the safer and happier we'll all be.

THIRTEEN

A Woman Describes the Negative Effects of the Sexual Harassment She Experienced in Her Youth

Danielle C. Belton

Danielle C. Belton is editor at large for *Clutch Magazine Online* and author of the blog *Black Snob*. Articles she has written include "What Makes Street Harassers Think Touching Is OK?" and "Bad Body Image Keeps Us from Enjoying Life." In the following viewpoint Belton shares what it was like for her to be sexually objectified by much older men from the age of twelve. According to Belton, the experience was quite traumatic, and for many years she hated her body and tried to hide it.

I have a big butt and I cannot lie. But goodness knows, for most of my life, I tried to deny it.

While some women dream of having kicking curves, for me there was a special horror having a big, round butt. Kids, thanks to other children, often loathe standing out, and my large posterior made me different. I was a stick skinny little kid and before starting school I simply thought my round booty was funny. I can remember looking at myself in the mirror around age 6, thinking I was shaped like a backward lower case "p." But that bemusement gave way to embarrassment by the time I was in the fourth grade. I suddenly took to pulling all my sweatshirts, T-shirts, and sweaters down as much as I could to cover my rear.

But I think I might have gotten over it—maybe—if having a big butt hadn't gone from goofy playground taunts to men three times my age licking their lips and shouting vulgarities at me when I was only 12 years old.

Sexually Objectified at a Young Age

At 12, sex (or being sexy) was the furthest thing from my mind. I still played with stuffed animals. I didn't like boys. And even though my mother sat me down and explained sex and puberty to me three years prior, none of it really clicked. Learning about human sexuality wasn't all that different from learning frog anatomy as far as I was concerned. It was just information. I hadn't processed it in any real way other than I understood that I now had to wear a training bra and suddenly deodorant was necessary.

So the first time someone started screaming about what they wanted to do with me sexually while I was in the food court of the old Northwest Plaza Mall in St. Louis County, I was frightened and confused. I looked to my mother—who was standing next to me—perplexed as to why this man and his friends were lewdly gesturing toward me and knowing it was terrifying, but she quickly told me to turn around and ignore it.

"They're ignorant," she said.

But she offered little explanation for what seemed dangerous and threatening. And it was around that age I started having nightmares about being physically assaulted by strangers or raped.

Traumatized by Repeated Harassment

In junior high, boys and the grown men they idolized (and who should have known better) were prone to shout just about anything at me. I think for them it was amusing, as I can only imagine what the success rate is for shouting at women and girls on

Overweight girls are often the targets of harassment, which can give a teen a bad body image.

the street, but when you're 12 or a teenager (or even now, to be honest) it's scary to have someone just announce that "you're so fine, if you were my daughter I'd have to rape you." The first boy to ever say this to me (we were both about 14) thought this was a "compliment." Even though I did my best to make it clear how

Students' Reactions to Sexual Harassment, by Gender

The graph depicts specific consequences experienced by students in grades seven to twelve who reported negative impacts from sexual harassment.

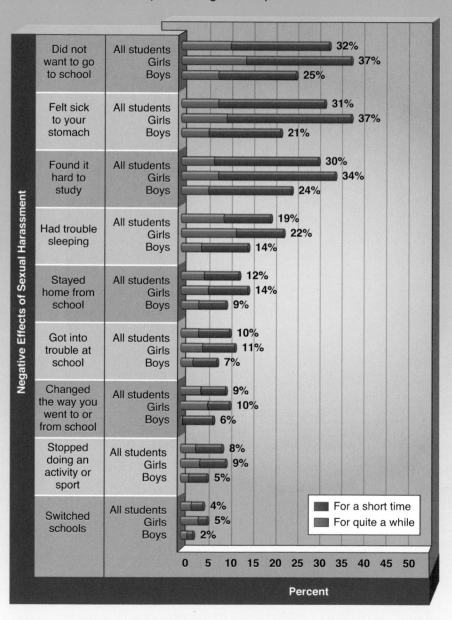

Negative Effects of Sexual Harassment

Did not want to go to school	All students	32%
	Girls	37%
	Boys	25%
Felt sick to your stomach	All students	31%
	Girls	37%
	Boys	21%
Found it hard to study	All students	30%
	Girls	34%
	Boys	24%
Had trouble sleeping	All students	19%
	Girls	22%
	Boys	14%
Stayed home from school	All students	12%
	Girls	14%
	Boys	9%
Got into trouble at school	All students	10%
	Girls	11%
	Boys	7%
Changed the way you went to or from school	All students	9%
	Girls	10%
	Boys	6%
Stopped doing an activity or sport	All students	8%
	Girls	9%
	Boys	5%
Switched schools	All students	4%
	Girls	5%
	Boys	2%

Percent: 0 5 10 15 20 25 30 35 40 45 50

Legend: For a short time / For quite a while

Taken from: Catherine Hill and Holly Kearl. *Crossing the Line: Sexual Harassment at School.* AAUW, November 2011. www.aauw.org/research/crossing–the–line/.

messed up that sounded, he insisted it was a funny joke he'd heard his uncle say to a girl and that I was way too uptight.

But it never seemed to stop. The vulgarities. The "friendly" stalking that ended with them cursing me out when I didn't want to give someone my number. This is pretty much why approaching a woman on the street if you're a halfway normal guy is almost pointless. By the time a woman is an adult, she's endured this kind of garbage for more than a decade and she just assumes you're a creep/potential rapist until you don't rape her. You honestly can't be mad at the woman for being traumatized. Be mad at the 40-year-old pervert who hit on her when she was 13.

As a woman you're told to just ignore or "deal" with street harassment (and all sexual harassment, honestly), so it is pretty easy to internalize it and think it's all your fault. For years I rued the day I hit puberty, seeing it as some horrible thing that made people suddenly go crazy on me. I wanted to stop whatever was causing this unwanted attention, meaning I often wore clothes two sizes too big for me.

This meant for years I didn't wear or even own a pair of shorts out of fear of showing my "big legs," which were obviously too provocative, even in Bermuda shorts or pedal pushers. My dream for the longest time was to be thin, really, really thin, size 0, smaller than small, thin. If I was just skinny enough that I had the body of a 10-year-old boy, I'd look more child-like and I wouldn't get so much unwanted sexual attention from men. The only problem was even if I got down to a size 4 or smaller in a shirt, I still wore pants that were a size 9/10 or larger.

So wearing my coat all day in the winter and blue jeans in the summer with long, loose fitting shirts was pretty much my look as I hated the body I was stuck with for a very long time.

The Path to Self-Acceptance

If I'm honest, I didn't fight through this physical self-loathing until I was 65 pounds heavier than I'd been in high school and 33 years old.

Yes. Thirty-three. As in the age I was last year [2011].

The road to physical self-acceptance was a long one, starting with realizing that part of the reason why I'd stopped doing my hair, gained so much weight and wore ever more baggy and unattractive clothes was because I didn't want anyone to bother me—ever. But as my depression lifted and I got back out into the world after losing most of my 20s to bipolar disorder, I went about learning how to dress (and accept) my body—giant butt and all. . . .

Realizing I had no control over what people do or say and letting that go was the biggest step of all. If men shout things, so what? They're the ones with the problem. They're the ones who are gross and rude. If anything, they make it easier to determine who I say hi to and who I cross the street to get away from. My giant butt doesn't make anyone do anything. Women trying to control their bodies in hopes of controlling a man's response is futile. After all, it wasn't like I was trying to entice or lead anyone on when I was 12 and wearing sack dresses and safari print short sets. Why punish myself and dress in a way that made me feel fat and frumpy and unfashionable to avoid some obnoxious, gross cat calls? Besides, like everyone in the history of the world, one day I'd grow old and would want to see pictures of me living my life and I'd think how great [I] looked, wondering why I didn't just enjoy myself and my youth instead of endlessly punishing myself for not being "perfect." I already do this with pictures from high school, questioning why I ever thought I was fat.

Surprisingly, the minute I accepted and, in turn, learned to love my body, I got over my phobia of exercise. I had given up on being in shape or exercising because I tied exercise to that dream of being prepubescent boy thin—something I could never be. So exercise filled me with hatred and self-loathing. But once I realized I liked my body and I liked the way I looked, it was super easy to go to the gym, be gross and sweaty, keep a diet, and keep off the weight. I've already lost 25 pounds and several inches. Instead of feeling anxiety about walking three miles or doing squats, I actually find myself looking forward to it and marveling at how strong I've become.

For the first time in my life, I don't feel any shame or fear about how I look. I feel good. And I feel positive. And my goals are realistic. I wish it hadn't taken so long, but the 12-year-old in me says it's better late than never.

What You Should Know About Sexual Harassment

Facts About Sexual Harassment

The American Association of University Women (AAUW) report *Crossing the Line: Sexual Harassment at School*, published in 2011, contains the following facts:

- Of surveyed students, during the 2010–2011 school year some type of sexual harassment was experienced by 56 percent of girls and 40 percent of boys in grades seven through twelve.
- Thirty-nine percent of boys and 62 percent of girls in grade twelve said they had experienced sexual harassment.
- Fifty-two percent of girls experienced harassment in person (as opposed to online), versus 35 percent of boys.
- Sexual harassment was witnessed by 33 percent of girls and 24 percent of boys during the 2010–2011 school year; of those who witnessed harassment, 56 percent did so on more than one occasion.
- Fourteen percent of girls and 18 percent of boys admitted to sexually harassing other students.
- Of students who admitted that they sexually harassed others:
  - 44 percent did not feel it was a big deal;
  - 39 percent said it was an attempt to be funny;
  - 23 percent said they did so as a form of retaliation for something previously done to them;
  - 6 percent believed the harassed person liked it;

- 3 percent wanted to date the person they harassed;
- 80 percent of male and 92 percent of female harassers had themselves been sexually harassed;
- 34 percent believed their behavior was stupid.
- Eighteen percent of both girls and boys said they were sexually harassed by being called lesbian or gay.
- Forty-six percent of girls experienced unwanted sexual jokes, comments, or gestures, compared with 22 percent of boys.
- Sixteen percent of girls were exposed to sexual images they did not wish to see, compared with 10 percent of boys.
- Three percent of boys and 13 percent of girls experienced unwanted sexual touching.
- Four percent of girls reported being forced to perform a sexual act, compared with 1 percent of boys.
- Seven percent of both girls and boys reported that another student indecently exposed her- or himself to them.
- Fifty-four percent of students reported being harassed by a lone male; 12 percent said they were harassed by a group of males.
- Fourteen percent said they were harassed by a lone female student; 5 percent reported harassment by a group of females.
- Eleven percent of those harassed said the perpetrators were a group of male and female students.
- Fifteen percent of students admitted to committing sexual harassment in person; 10 percent said they had done so via electronic media (e-mail, Facebook, texting, etc.).
- Of male students who admitted to sexually harassing others, 72 percent said they did so to another boy, compared with 19 percent who did so to a girl.
- Of female students who admitted to sexually harassing others, 50 percent said they did so to a boy whereas 41 percent said they harassed another girl.
- Asked who was more likely to be a target of sexual harassment:
  - 37 percent said boys who were not considered very "masculine" or athletic;
  - 11 percent said boys who were physically attractive;

- 58 percent said girls whose bodies were more sexually mature;
- 41 percent said girls who are physically attractive;
- 32 percent said girls who are not considered very "feminine" or pretty;
- 30 percent said overweight boys or girls.
- Ninety percent of students indicated that they know it is unacceptable to tease girls who act in a way considered masculine or boys who act in a way considered feminine.
- Ninety-one percent of students know that those targeted for sexual harassment are not to blame.

The report *Harassment-Free Hallways: How to Stop Sexual Harassment in School*, published by the AAUW in 2004, notes that

- 91.5 percent of LGBT (lesbian, gay, bisexual, and transgender) students said they often or frequently hear homophobic comments at school.
- 82.9 percent of LGBT students say school faculty members who overhear such comments never or only sometimes intervene.

According to *LGBT Related Sexual Harassment in School*, a report prepared by Lynda M. Sagrestano for the University of Memphis in 2009:

- 26.1 percent of students were called lesbian or gay in school—12.4 percent once, and 13.7 percent two or more times;
- 31.7 percent of boys were so labeled, compared with 23.9 percent of girls;
- 4.9 percent of students were called lesbian or gay by an adult in school.

Two informal online surveys done by Holly Kearl in 2007 and 2008, as reported by the organization Stop Street Harassment, report that 99 percent of respondents (including a few males) in the 2007 survey reported being sexually harassed; more than 65 percent said they experienced harassment at least once per month.

In the 2008 survey, more than 99 percent of the 916 respondents (all female) reported experiencing sexual harassment on the street ("street harassment"). Of those,

- 95 percent experienced excessive staring/leering on at least 1 occasion whereas 68 percent experienced it at least 26 times;
- almost 95 percent said they were honked at at least 1 time, with 40 percent reporting experiencing it monthly;
- about 94 percent were whistled at on at least 1 occasion, with 38 percent experiencing it monthly;
- more than 87 percent were targeted by sexist comments at least 1 time; 45 percent have experienced it 25 times or more;
- vulgar gestures were directed at about 82 percent of the women on at least 1 occasion, with approximately 20 percent experiencing it 51 times or more;
- strangers directed sexually explicit comments at almost 81 percent of the women at least 1 time whereas 41 percent of the respondents experienced it 26 times or more;
- men made kissing noises to more than 77 percent of the respondents, with 48 percent experiencing it 25 times or more;
- strangers followed 75 percent of the women in public at least 1 time, with over 27 percent experiencing this 6 times or more;
- a man deliberately blocked the path of 62 percent of the women at least 1 time whereas 23 percent of women have experienced this 6 times or more;
- almost 57 percent of the respondents have had a stranger grab or touch them in a sexual manner in public while approximately 18 percent had this happen 6 times or more;
- a stranger masturbated at or near more than 37 percent of the women on at least 1 occasion;
- approximately 27 percent of the women said they were assaulted by a stranger in public at least 1 time.

- an e-mail, post, or text message with unwanted sexual jokes, pictures, or comments was seen by 20 percent of students in the 2010–2011 school year;
- being called lesbian or gay as an insult via e-mail, texting, or other digital means was experienced by 12 percent of students;
- 13 percent of students were the target of online sexual rumors.

According to a report issued in 2013 by Working to Halt Online Abuse (WHO@) that compiled statistics from 2000 to 2012:

- 72.5 percent of victims of online harassment/cyberstalking were female, 22.5 percent were male, and 5 percent were of unknown gender;
- 47.5 percent of online harassers were male, 30.25 percent were female, 1.25 percent were multiple/gangs, and 21 percent were of unknown gender;
- 49.25 percent of online harassers had a relationship with their victims, 49.75 percent did not, and in 1 percent of cases it is not known whether there was a relationship;
- harassment began via e-mail in 35.25 percent of cases, via message board in 13 percent of cases, via instant messaging (IM) in 11.5 percent of cases, via chat in 8 percent of cases, via a website in 7.75 percent of cases, and via Facebook in 3.5 percent of cases, whereas harassment beginning via phone, MySpace, dating, Craigslist, texting, or gaming occurred in less than 2 percent of cases each;
- 60.25 percent of harassment cases were escalated online, and 21.5 percent of cases included offline threats;
- victims reported the harassment in 54.25 percent of cases.

Effects of Sexual Harassment

The AAUW's report *Crossing the Line: Sexual Harassment at School* discloses the following:

- Eighty-seven percent of the students in grades seven through twelve who had experienced sexual harassment reported that it had a negative impact.

- More girls than boys reported negative effects from sexual harassment; such effects included:
    - difficulty sleeping (22 percent of girls; 14 percent of boys);
    - desire to not go back to school (37 percent of girls, 25 percent of boys);
    - wanting to change their route to/from school (10 percent of girls, 6 percent of boys);
    - feeling nauseated by the harassment they experienced (37 percent of girls, 21 percent of boys);
    - difficulty studying (34 percent of girls, 24 percent of boys);
    - quitting a sport or activity (8 percent of students).
- Asked what types of sexual harassment had the greatest negative effect on them
    - 36 percent of girls and 16 percent of boys said unwanted sexual gestures, comments, or jokes;
    - 17 percent of girls and 11 percent of boys said being the target of online sexual rumors;
    - 9 percent of girls and 21 percent of boys said being called lesbian or gay.
- Forty-six percent of students who experienced sexual harassment both in person and online did not want to go back to school because of it, whereas only 19 percent of students who only experienced it in person and 18 percent who only experienced it online did not want to return to school.
- Forty-three percent of students who were harassed both in person and online found it difficult to focus on their studies because of the harassment whereas 17 percent who had experienced harassment only online or only in person had such difficulty.

Response to Sexual Harassment

The AAUW's report *Crossing the Line: Sexual Harassment at School* relates the following:

- Of surveyed students in grades seven through twelve who were the target of sexual harassment,
    - 12 percent of girls and 5 percent of boys told a guidance counselor, teacher, or other school faculty/staff member;
    - 32 percent of girls and 20 percent of boys spoke with parents, siblings, or other family members;
    - 29 percent of girls and 15 percent of boys talked to friends about the incident(s);
    - 13 percent of boys and 31 percent of girls told those harassing them to stop;
    - 11 percent of girls and 22 percent of boys tried to defuse the situation with humor;
    - 44 percent of girls and 59 percent of boys did nothing about being harassed.
- Seventeen percent of boys and 24 percent of girls attempted to help a student they saw being harassed.
- Sixty-eight percent of those who tried to come to the aid of another student being harassed had themselves experienced sexual harassment.
- Of students who helped others who were being harassed,
    - 60 percent told those committing the harassment to stop;
    - 54 percent asked the harassed student whether they were alright;
    - 24 percent told a guidance counselor, teacher, or other faculty/staff member about the incident(s);
    - 22 percent reported it to their parents or another family member.
- Of those students who saw sexual harassment happening but took no action,
    - 36 percent were not sure what to do;
    - 28 percent did not believe they could help the situation;
    - 26 percent did not realize it was sexual harassment when it happened;
    - 13 percent feared they would be harassed if they intervened;

- 9 percent feared they would be physically hurt by the harassers if they interfered.
- Only 12 percent of students believed their school was adequately dealing with sexual harassment and gave the following suggestions to improve the situation:
    - schools should identify a specific person to talk to about harassment (39 percent);
    - schools should offer resources online (22 percent);
    - schools should have discussions in class (31 percent);
    - schools should provide a way to report incidents anonymously (57 percent);
    - schools should punish harassers (51 percent).

A *Washington Post*–ABC News poll conducted in 2011 reported the following:

- Only 36 percent of people who experienced sexual harassment at work reported the incident(s) to their employer.
- Of those who did not inform their employer, the reasons given for not reporting included the following:
    - 31 percent felt it was "not important enough";
    - 22 percent felt it "wouldn't do any good"; and
    - 18 percent were "concerned about consequences."
- Of women who either were never harassed, or were but did not report it, 56 percent believed that if they had reported it, the case would have been dealt with fairly; 32 percent believed it would not have been dealt with fairly.

What You Should Do About Sexual Harassment

Get Informed

The first step in grappling with any complex and controversial issue is to be informed about it. Gather as much information as you can from a variety of sources. The essays in this book form an excellent starting point, representing a variety of viewpoints and approaches to the topic. Your school or local library will be another source of useful information; look there for relevant books, magazines, and encyclopedia entries. The bibliography and list of organizations to contact in this book will give you useful starting points in gathering additional information.

There is a wealth of information and perspectives on sexual harassment in the US, Canadian, and international media. Internet search engines will be helpful to you in your research. Many blogs and websites have information and articles dealing with the topic from a variety of perspectives, including concerned individuals offering their opinions, activist organizations, governmental organizations such as the US Department of Education Office for Civil Rights (OCR), and popular media outlets.

Many articles, books, and other resources that deal with the topic have been published in recent years. Academic papers and reports on sexual harassment are also available. If the information in such papers is too dense or technical, check the abstract at the beginning of the article, which provides a clear summary of the researcher's conclusions.

You may also want to find and interview people who have experienced sexual harassment firsthand or who have worked with those who have been targeted by sexual harassment. There are websites and organizations that publish sexual harassment narratives and help people who have experienced it. Such groups can be contacted by phone or via the Internet (start with the organizations to contact in this book).

Identify the Issues

Once you have gathered your information, analyze it to discover the key issues involved. What causes sexual harassment? Who is affected by it? What forms does sexual harassment take? Is there a difference between sexual harassment and rape or sexual assault, or is rape/sexual assault a particularly severe form of sexual harassment? What psychological and emotional effects does sexual harassment have on those targeted by it and on those who witness it happening to others? What can or should be done to deal with sexual harassment by those targeted, by witnesses, by the legal system or the culture at large? How has modern technology such as the Internet and smartphones affected the landscape of sexual harassment?

It may be worthwhile to consider how sexual harassment has developed—and been dealt with—in other cultures and time periods, to get a broader perspective on what is happening in North America today. For example, since 2006, sexual harassment has become a big issue in Egypt, with much media attention both in that country and around the world. India is another nation that has recently had a great deal of media attention and popular protest focused on sexual harassment.

Evaluate Your Information Sources

In developing your own opinion, it is vital to evaluate the sources of the information you have discovered. Authors of books, magazine articles, etc., however well-intentioned, have their own perspectives and biases, which may affect how they present information on the subject. Sexual harassment is a contentious issue, and people have very different ways of looking at and evaluating it. In some cases people and organizations may deliberately or inadvertently distort information to support a strongly held ideological or moral position—signs of this include oversimplification and extreme positions.

Consider the authors' credentials and what organizations they are affiliated with. You may find that approaches to dealing with sexual harassment vary depending on the beliefs of the people or agencies involved. If you find someone arguing against his or her expected bias—for example, a feminist arguing that sexual harassment legislation has gone too far, or a men's rights activist arguing that men need to take more responsibility for their behavior, it may be worthwhile to pay particular attention to their arguments. Always critically evaluate and assess your sources rather than take whatever they say at face value.

Examine Your Own Perspective

Sexual harassment is a complex and emotionally charged topic. Spend some time exploring your own thoughts and feelings about it. Consider the attitudes and beliefs about this issue that you have received from family members, friends, and the media throughout your life. Such messages affect your own thoughts and feelings about the subject. Have you or anyone you know ever experienced or been accused of sexual harassment? If so, that may make it more challenging to form a clear view of the issues involved, and/or it may give you special insight into the topic. Be wary of "confirmation bias," the tendency to seek out information that confirms what you already believe to be true, and to discount information that contradicts your beliefs. Deliberately counter this tendency by seeking out perspectives that contradict your current opinions.

Form Your Own Opinion and Take Action

Once you have gathered and organized information, identified the issues involved, and examined your own perspective, you will be ready to form an opinion on sexual harassment and to advocate your position in debates and discussions (and if you or someone close to you is having difficulties with sexual harassment, you will have a better idea of what resources and approaches are available to deal with the problem). Perhaps you will conclude that one of the viewpoints you have encountered offers the best explanation of sexual harassment and what to do about it, or you may decide that a number of approaches working together are needed to adequately address this complex issue. You might even decide that none of the perspectives on sexual harassment that you have encountered are convincing to you and that you cannot take a decisive position as yet. If that is the case, ask yourself what you would need to know to make up your mind; perhaps a bit more research would be helpful. Whatever position you take, be prepared to explain it clearly on the basis of facts, evidence, and well-thought-out beliefs.

ORGANIZATIONS TO CONTACT

The editors have compiled the following list of organizations concerned with the issues debated in this book. The descriptions are derived from materials provided by the organizations. All have publications or information available for interested readers. The list was compiled on the date of publication of the present volume; names, addresses, phone and fax numbers, and e-mail and Internet addresses may change. Be aware that many organizations take several weeks or longer to respond to inquiries, so allow as much time as possible.

American Association of University Women (AAUW)
1111 Sixteenth St. NW
Washington, DC 20036
(202) 785-7700 • fax: (202) 872-1425
e-mail: connect@aauw.org
website: www.aauw.org

Founded in 1881, the AAUW is a leading voice promoting equity and education for women and girls. This nonprofit grassroots organization comprises more than 165,000 members and supporters, one thousand local branches, and eight hundred college and university partners. The AAUW has produced a number of influential reports on sexual harassment (available for download on its website), including *Drawing the Line: Sexual Harassment on Campus, Crossing the Line: Sexual Harassment at School,* and *Hostile Hallways: Bullying, Teasing, and Sexual Harassment in School.* The AAUW maintains a presence on Facebook, Twitter, Tumblr, and YouTube and features a "get involved" page on its website listing ten ways people can get involved in furthering its mission.

American Civil Liberties Union (ACLU)
125 Broad St., 18th Fl.
New York, NY 10004

(212) 549-2500
website: www.aclu.org

The ACLU works daily in courts, legislatures, and communities to defend and preserve the individual rights and liberties that the Constitution and laws of the United States guarantee everyone. A search on the organization's website for "sexual harassment" yields many results, including the 2011 report *Gender-Based Violence & Harassment: Your School, Your Rights* and *The Cost of Harassment: A Fact Sheet for Lesbian, Gay, Bisexual and Transgender High School Students*.

Feminist Majority Foundation (FMF)
1600 Wilson Blvd., Ste. 801
Arlington, VA 22209
(703) 522-2214 • fax: (703) 522-2219
website: www.feminist.org

The FMF is an organization founded in 1987 that is dedicated to promoting women's equality, reproductive health, and safety. The FMF seeks to empower women economically, socially, and politically through research and public policy development, public education programs, grassroots organizing projects, and leadership training and development programs. Its website provides resources and hotlines for dealing with sexual harassment and sexual assault, as well as videos, a blog, reports, and fact sheets on feminist issues.

Girls for Gender Equity (GGE)
30 Third Ave., Ste. 103
Brooklyn, NY 11217
(718) 857-1393 • fax: (718) 857-2239
email: Info@ggenyc.org
website: www.ggenyc.org

GGE is a nonprofit organization that is committed to the physical, psychological, social, and economic development of girls and women. Through education, organizing, and physical fitness, GGE encourages communities to remove barriers and create opportunities for girls and women to live self-determined lives. Its website has a section on sexual harassment and offers the newsletter *GGE Friends*. GGE publishes *Hey, Shorty! A Guide to Combating Sexual Harassment and Violence in Schools and on the Streets*.

HollaBack!
30 Third Ave., #800B
Brooklyn, NY 11217
(347) 889-5510
e-mail: holla@ihollaback.org
website: www.ihollaback.org

Hollaback! is a nonprofit organization leading a global movement to end street harassment. A network of local activists around the world collaborate to better understand street harassment, ignite public conversations, and develop innovative strategies to ensure equal access to public spaces. Hollaback! has empowered people in over fifty cities and twenty countries to respond through a smartphone app. Users are encouraged to speak up when they see harassment by quickly documenting it in a short post (photo optional) and sharing it to a publicly viewable map. The Hollaback! website features stories of harassment and efforts to counteract harassment from around the world. The website's resources page includes book recommendations, articles, videos, how-to guides, research, and Android and iPhone apps to download.

Man Up Campaign
79 Fifth Ave., 4th Fl.
New York, NY 10003
(646) 862-2854
website: http://manupcampaign.org

The Man Up Campaign aims to engage youth in a global movement to end gender-based violence and advance gender equality through youth-led initiatives intended to transform communities, nations, and the world by promoting gender equality and sensitivity among youth and building a community of like-minded individuals, initiatives, and organizations. Issues addressed include sexual harassment, psychological and emotional abuse, and rape. Man Up Campaign maintains a presence on Twitter, Facebook, and YouTube. Visitors to its website can register to be notified of events, information, and opportunities in their country.

Men Can Stop Rape (MCSR)
1003 K St. NW, Ste. 200
Washington, DC 20001
(202) 265-6530 • fax: (202) 265-4362
e-mail: info@mencanstoprape.org
website: www.mencanstoprape.org

MCSR is a nonprofit organization based in Washington, D.C., whose mission is to mobilize men to use their strength for creating cultures free from violence, especially male violence against women. Rather than helping women reduce their risk of being victims of male violence, the organization focuses on helping boys and men use their strength in positive ways in all of their relationships. MCSR founded the Men of Strength Club (MOST Club), a school-based twenty-two-week curriculum teaching males aged eleven to eighteen healthy dating and relationship skills and encouraging them to show their "strength" in positive ways among their peers. It also distributes posters and other information designed to empower middle-school-aged boys to take action against gender-based harassment, teasing, bullying, and cyberbullying. The MCSR website offers a newsletter, news items, videos, and handouts.

National Organization for Women (NOW)
1100 H St. NW, Ste. 300
Washington, D.C. 20005
(202) 628-8669
website: http://now.org

NOW is the largest organization of feminist activists in the United States, claiming five hundred thousand contributing members and 550 chapters in all fifty states and the District of Columbia. Since its founding in 1966, NOW's goal has been to take action to bring about equality for all women. NOW works to eliminate discrimination and harassment in the workplace, schools, the justice system, and all other sectors of society; to end all forms of violence against women; to eradicate racism, sexism, and homophobia; and to promote equality and justice. The organization's website includes ways to take action, news bulletins, and the *Say It, Sister!* blog. Visitors can sign up for several e-mail newsletters, including *Action Alerts*, *News and Action Summary*, and *News Releases*. Searching "sexual harassment" on the NOW website yields hundreds of results.

Rape, Abuse, and Incest National Network (RAINN)
1220 L St., NW, Ste. 505
Washington, DC 20005
(202) 544-3064 • fax: (202) 544-3556
e-mail: info@rainn.org
website: www.rainn.org

RAINN is the nation's largest anti-sexual-violence organization and was named one of "America's 100 Best Charities" by *Worth* magazine. RAINN created and operates the National Sexual Assault Hotline (800-656-HOPE and online.rainn.org) in partnership with more than eleven hundred local rape crisis centers across the United States. RAINN also carries out programs to prevent sexual violence, help victims of sexual violence, and ensure that rapists are brought to justice. The organization's website includes information on reducing the risk of sexual assault, recovering from sexual violence, and computer safety.

US Department of Education Office for Civil Rights (OCR)
1990 K St. NW
Washington, DC 20006
(800) 872-5327
website: www2.ed.gov/about/offices/list/ocr

The US Department of Education OCR is responsible for ensuring that educational institutions that receive federal funding (as most do) comply with Title IX, the federal law prohibiting sex discrimination, including sexual harassment. Educational institutions overseen by the OCR are required to have a designated Title IX coordinator. Sexual harassment resources can be found on the OCR website, including "Know Your Rights: Title IX Prohibits Sexual Harassment and Sexual Violence Where You Go to School," "Frequently Asked Questions About Sexual Harassment" and "Checklist for Addressing Harassment."

US Equal Employment Opportunity Commission (EEOC)
131 M St. NE
Washington, DC 20507
(202) 663-4900
e-mail: info@eeoc.gov
website: www.eeoc.gov

The EEOC enforces federal laws that make it illegal to discriminate against a job applicant or an employee on the basis of sex, race, color, religion, national origin, disability, or genetic information. The laws apply to all types of work situations, including hiring, firing, promotions, harassment, training, wages, and benefits. Its website's section on Sexual Harassment includes facts about sexual harassment, information on relevant regulations, how to file a charge of discrimination, and statistics. Searching for "sexual harassment" on the site returns thousands of results.

BIBLIOGRAPHY

Books

Gavin de Becker, *The Gift of Fear and Other Survival Signals That Protect Us from Violence*. Boston: Little, Brown, 1997.

Heather Corinna, *S.E.X.: The All-You-Need-to-Know Progressive Sexuality Guide to Get You Through High School and College*. New York: Marlowe, 2007.

Esther Drill, Heather McDonald, and Rebecca Odes, *Deal with It! A Whole New Approach to Your Body, Brain, and Life*. New York: Pocket, 1999.

Nanette Gartrell, *My Answer Is No—If That's OK with You: How Women Can Say NO and (Still) Feel Good About It*. New York: Free Press, 2008.

Robie H. Harris and Michael Emberley, *It's Perfectly Normal: Changing Bodies, Growing Up, Sex, and Sexual Health*. Somerville, MA: Candlewick, 2009.

Holly Kearl, *Stop Street Harassment: Making Public Places Safe and Welcoming for Women*. Santa Barbara, CA: Praeger, 2010.

Courtney Macavinta and Andrea R. Pluym, *Respect: A Girl's Guide to Getting Respect & Dealing When Your Line Is Crossed*. Minneapolis: Free Spirit, 2005.

Kathleen Parker, *Save the Males: Why Men Matter; Why Women Should Care*. New York: Random House, 2008.

Matt Posner and Jess C. Scott, *Teen Guide to Sex and Relationships*. Maine: jessINK, 2012.

Joanne N. Smith, Mandy van Deven, and Meghan Huppuch, *Hey, Shorty! A Guide to Combating Sexual Harassment and Violence in Schools and on the Streets*. New York: Feminist, 2011.

Susan Strauss, *Sexual Harassment and Bullying: A Guide to Keeping Kids Safe and Holding Schools Accountable*. Lanham, MD: Rowman & Littlefield, 2012.

Jennie Withers and Phyllis Hendrickson, *Hey, Back Off!: Tips for Stopping Teen Harassment*. Far Hills, NJ: New Horizon, 2011.

Irene van der Zande, *Bullying: What Adults Need to Know and Do to Keep Kids Safe*. Santa Cruz, CA: Kidpower, 2010.

Periodicals and Internet Sources

Arthur Dobrin, "Hugging Will Get You in Trouble: Everyone Needs to Be Touched," *Psychology Today*, November 12, 2011.

Cath Elliott, "So Angry I Could Strip!, *Guardian* (Manchester, UK), May 28, 2008. www.guardian.co.uk/commentisfree/2008/may/28/soangryicouldstrip.

James Fletcher, "Sexual Harassment in the World of Video Gaming," BBC, June 3, 2012. www.bbc.co.uk/news/magazine-18280000.

Ozy Frantz, "Sexual Harassment Policies on Campus," Good Men Project, March 1, 2012. http://goodmenproject.com/sexism/sexual-harassment-policies-on-campus.

Julie Gerstein, "Yes, Men—Like Danny Brown—Can Be Victims of Sexual Assault, Too," Frisky, May 2, 2013. www.thefrisky.com/2013-05-02/yes-men-like-danny-brown-can-be-victims-of-sexual-assault-too.

Samara Ginsberg, "Women Have Boobs—Get Over It," AlterNet, February 3, 2009. www.alternet.org/story/125164/women_have_boobs_--_get_over_it?paging=off.

Carlos Andrés Gómez, "Why Men Catcall," Good Men Project, September 16, 2012. http://goodmenproject.com/ethics-values/why-men-catcall.

Nat Guest, "Only 4 in 10? We Should Speak Up About Harassment, *Independent* (London), blogs, May 25, 2012. http://blogs.independent.co.uk/2012/05/25/only-4-in-10-we-should-speak-up-about-harassment.

Amanda Hess, "The UnSlut Project Is the 'It Gets Better' of Slut-Shaming," XX Factor, April 26, 2013. www.slate.com/blogs/xx_factor/2013/04/26/the_unslut_project_a_new_tumblr_is_the_it_gets_better_of_slut_shaming.html.

Paul Joannides, "The Double Standard in Sexting," *Psychology Today*, April 10, 2010.

Holly Kearl, "Feeling Harassed? Do Something About It," *Guardian* (Manchester, UK), August 26, 2011. www.guardian.co.uk/com mentisfree/cifamerica/2011/aug/26/sexual-harassment-women -equality.

Holly Kearl, "2012 #ENDSH Successes Part 5: Twenty-Five Stories," Stop Street Harassment, December 28, 2012. www .stopstreetharassment.org/2012/12/annualroundup5.

Genevieve LeBlanc, "Sexual Harassment in the Convention Community: A Personal Account," Nerd Reactor, November 14, 2012. http://nerdreactor.com/2012/11/14/sexual-harassment -in-the-convention-community-a-personal-account/

Alison Rose Levy, "Are Patdowns Sexual Harassment?, *Psychology Today*, November 26, 2010.

National Public Radio, "Teen Sexual Assault: Where Does the Conversation Start?," April 28, 2013. www.wbur.org /npr/179671126/teen-sexual-assault-where-does-the-conversa tion-start.

Jennifer P., "Reader Question #78: Honor Students Can Also Be Inappropriate Assholes," Captain Awkward, July 24, 2011. http://captainawkward.com/2011/07/24/reader-question -78-honor-students-can-also-be-inappropriate-assholes.

Abigail Pesta, "'Thanks for Ruining My Life,'" *Daily Beast*, December 12, 2012. www.thedailybeast.com/newsweek/2012/12/09/thanks -for-ruining-my-life.html.

Almie Rose, "Stop Hitting on Me," Apocalypstick, August 10, 2010. http://apocalypstick.com/stop-hitting-on-me.

Alyssa Rosenberg, "Men Are More Sensitive to Rape Jokes than Women, *Vanity Fair* Poll Finds," Think Progress, December 5, 2012. http://thinkprogress.org/alyssa/2012/12/05/1283761 /vanity-fair-poll-men-are-more-sensitive-to-rape-jokes-than -women/?mobile=nc.

Anita Sarkeesian, "Image Based Harassment and Visual Misogyny," Feminist Frequency, July 1, 2012. www.feministfrequency .com/2012/07/image-based-harassment-and-visual-misogyny.

Brigid Schulte, "For Little Children, Grown-Up Labels as Sexual Harassers," *Washington Post*, April 3, 2008. www.washingtonpost.com/wp-dyn/content/article/2008/04/02/AR2008040203463.html.

Hugo Schwyzer, "'Slut-Shaming Fatigue': Because This Crap Has Got to Stop," Jezebel, January 28, 2013. http://jezebel.com/5978766/slut+shaming-fatigue-because-this-nonsense-has-got-to-stop.

Emily Smith, "Your Take: What's Behind Street Harassment?," CNN, October 10, 2012. www.cnn.com/2012/10/10/living/street-harassment-overheard.

S.E. Smith, "Why We Judge Sexual Harassment Victims, plus the Time I Got Drive-by Oinked At," XO Jane, November 12, 2012. www.xojane.com/issues/surprise-were-judgy-about-sexual-harassment-victims-because-we-think-we-wouldnt-be-as-passive.

Christina Hoff Sommers, "Crying Wolf: Feminist Sexual-Harassment Hysteria," *National Review*, February 21, 2006.

Kathryn Stamoulis, "'Hey Baby' Hurts: The Psychological Implications of Street Harassment," *Psychology Today*, August 19, 2011.

Ferrett Steinmetz, "Look, Guys, Even 'Nice' Can Be Annoying," Jezebel, October 23, 2012. http://jezebel.com/5953909/look-guys-even-nice-can-be-annoying?tag=harassment.

Jessica Valenti, "Is Segregation the Only Answer to Sexual Harassment?," *Guardian* (Manchester, UK), August 2, 2007. www.guardian.co.uk/lifeandstyle/2007/aug/03/healthandwellbeing.gender.

Susan Walsh, "Katie Roiphe Talks Sense About Sexual Harassment," Hooking Up Smart, November 17, 2011. www.hookingupsmart.com/2011/11/17/politics-and-feminism/katie-roiphe-talks-sense-about-sexual-harassment.

Vic Walter, "Starbucks Settles with Teen Barista Over 'Sex Demands' at Work," ABC News, June 4, 2010. http://abcnews.go.com/Blotter/Teen/starbucks-settles-teen-barista-sex-demands-work/story?id=10827639#.UYBJjEBDutU.

Plautus, Titus, 60, 66
Polls. *See* Surveys
Prevention
  schools efforts at,
    35–39
  through mobile online
    technology, 5, 46–51
Prince, Phoebe, 31, 32
Public sexual harassment
  is problem requiring legal
    regulation, 52–56
  origins of slang terms
    related to, 62
  percentage of women
    having experienced, by
    city/country, 79

Q
Quinn, Beth A., 61

R
Rape
  attitudes on jokes about,
    69
  as constant threat to
    women, 63–64
Reid, Oraia, 48
Rose, Almie, 65

S
Sarkeesian, Anita,
  6–8
Schiesel, Seth, 8

Schools
  attempts to solve sexual
    harassment problem in,
    35–39
  prevalence of sexual
    harassment in, 11
  role in preventing sexual
    harassment, 15–16
  sexual harassment is
    serious problem in,
    30–34
  student suggestions
    for reducing sexual
    harassment in, by gender,
    33
Schwyzer, Hugo, 77
Self image, impact of
  sexual harassment on,
    87–88
Sexual harassers, women
  need to confront,
    57–66
Sexual harassment
  categories of, 5, 11–12
  charges for, percentage
    filed by males, 75
  definition of, 11–12
  effects on students,
    13–15
  is about power, 24–29
  is serious problem in
    schools, 30–34
  male-to-male, as abuse
    of power in workplace,
    71–76

men need to take role in ending, 67–70

negative effects on students, by gender, 86

notable penalties for employers charged with, 37

percentage of college students having experienced, by sexual identity, 29

personal account of woman's experience in youth, 83–88

prevalence of, 11, 54, 64

underreporting of, 15

women's dress does not contribute to, 77–82

See also Online sexual harassment; Prevention; Public sexual harassment

Sexual Harassment and Masculinity (Quinn), 61

Spodak, Cassie, 46

Street harassment. See Public sexual harassment

Students

college, percentage experiencing sexual harassment, 29

effects of sexual harassment on, 13–15, 86

suggestions of, for reducing sexual harassment in school, 33

Suicide, of Phoebe Prince, 32

Sundowner Offshore Services, Oncale v. (1998), 74

Surveys

on amount of time men/women spend staring at each other, 20

of attitudes on rape/sexual assault jokes, 69

of college students experiencing sexual harassment, 29

on prevalence of street harassment, 54

on sexual harassment in Egypt, 56

of women, strangers who harass, 64

Sydney Morning Herald (newspaper), 78

T

Teachers, hesitate to intervene in sexual harassment, 34

Thomas, Clarence, 72

Tiller, Rob, 81

Timmerman, G., 32

Title VII (Civil Rights Act of 1964), 53